A Book of Odes

Nishi Kanta Sarkar

A BOOK OF ODES

First published in 2017 by

Becomeshakespeare.com
Wordit Content Design & Editing Services Pvt. Ltd.
Unit - 26, Building A-1, Nr Wadala RTO, Wadala (East),
Mumbai 400037, India
T:+91 8080226699

Wordit Art Fund helps deserving authors publish their work by providing monetary support. To apply for funding, please visit us at
www.BecomeShakespeare.com

Copyright © 2017 by Nishi Kanta Sarkar

All rights reserved. Any unauthorized reprint or use of this material is prohibited. No part of this book may be reproduced or transmitted in any form or by any means, electronic or mechanical, including photocopying, recording, or by any information storage and retrieval system without express written permission from the author/publisher.
Please do not participate in or encourage piracy of copyrighted materials in violation of the author's rights. Purchase only authorized editions.

©
ISBN 978-93-86487-77-3

DEDICATION

Dedicated to the sacred memory of my beloved mother-
Who nourished my heart in such an ecstatic manner-
That it blossoms into a flower of pink and pearl-
Which induces me to serve the suppressed humanity,
With divine love and filial piety.

A BOOK OF ODES

ACKNOWLEDGMENTS

I was greatly influenced by the poem 'The Solitary Reaper' of William Wordsworth which inspired me to write my first poem 'The Green Lady'.

I sincerely acknowledge the inspiration and continuous encouragement of my friends, colleagues and other well-wishers.

I am thankful to the members of my family for their love and sacrifice without which 'a book of odes' may not see the light of the day.

I am grateful to the Management and Staff of the Wordit Content Design and Editing Services Pvt. Ltd. and Leadstart Publishing Pvt. Ltd. for their support and continuous active services in publishing this book within the shortest period of time.

PROLOGUE

This book is borne out of a desire to find out a better way to clothe my leisure hours with creative imagination and on the other hand to lead my solitary life with ease and abundance.

A BRIEF HISTORY OF THE ODES

The word 'ode' is Greek in origin. It comes from the Greek word 'Aeido' meaning to sing. Actually, 'ode' is a lyrical poem of exalted style and tone and often of varied or irregular metre. The 'ode' maybe called a poetic oration. Being a sub division of the lyric, the 'ode' is lyrical in essence. It may be personal in inspiration or it may be purely objective in nature.

Odes were first written by 'Pindar', an ancient Greek poet. The Pindaric ode consists of a composition unit of a three stages termed as "strophe, anti-strophe and epode". This unit being repeated until the poem is complete .The pattern of the Pindaric ode is very complex and intricate. Another classical variety of the 'ode' was originated by Horace, an ancient roman poet. The Horatian ode uses a particular stanza throughout and there is no intricacy in this form of ode.

Although both the Pindaric and the Horatian odes have been written in English also. Most of the English writers of the ode have ignored the patterns of Pindar and Horace so that their odes show a complete liberty of rhyme and stanza. Indeed any impassioned English poem of unsystematic rhyme, rhythm and metre maybe called an 'ode'. Under the control of 'genius', this kind of irregular ode has resulted in some of the finest poems in English.

CONTENTS

ODE TO THE GREEN LADY 14

ODE ON CHARACTER.. 16

ODE ON THE DEVOTED LOVERS.. 18

ODE ON THE DESERT 20

ODE ON A LOVELESS LIFE.. 21

ODE ON THE DESIRE 22

ODE ON THE NOBLE HERITAGE 23

ODE ON DUTY 25

ODE ON POVERTY.. 26

ODE ON A LIFE LONG PRISONER.. 28

ODE ON AN UNKNOWN BOATMAN 30

ODE ON A FLOWERY BOWER... 31

ODE ON THE HAPPINESS 32

ODE TO THE MOTHERLAND... 34

ODE ON BEAUTY 35

ODE TO THE APRIL SUN	36
ODE ON THE FEIGNING FRIENDSHIP	37
ODE TO THE BELOVED 'SHE'	38
ODE ON THE MILLENNIUM	39
ODE ON A SAD BEREAVEMENT	40
ODE ON LOVE	41
ODE ON THE BLACK CURTAIN	42
ODE ON TIME	43
ODE ON THE SOLITARY LOVER	44
ODE ON THE PSALM OF LIFE	46
ODE ON A NEGLECTED FLOWER	47
ODE ON LUCY	48
ODE ON THE UNIVERSAL FRATERNITY	49
ODE ON THE DEATHLESS LIFE	50
ODE ON POLLUTION	51
ODE ON THE NIGHT QUEEN	52
ODE ON WATER	53
ODE ON OLD MONKEY	55
ODE ON MRS. WHITE	57
ODE ON THE MEMORIAL	58
ODE ON THE GUIDING SPIRIT	59
ODE ON THE GREAT GRANDMOTHER	60
ODE ON THE NEWBORN BABY	61

ODE ON THE RETURN JOURNEY	62
ODE ON THE BOSOM FRIEND	64
ODE ON THE CREATIVITY OF LIFE	65
ODE ON PEACE	66
ODE ON WAR	67
ODE TO THE SELFISH MAN	69
ODE ON THE CAGED LIFE	71
ODE ON A SONG	72
ODE ON THE MOSQUITO	73
ODE ON A ROSE	74
ODE ON A PET	75
ODE ON THE CLARION CALL	76
ODE ON A GREEN COCONUT	77
ODE TO THE ALMIGHTY FATHER	78
ODE ON A HIGHLAND LASS	79
ODE ON A WHITE LADY	80
ODE ON ENJOYMENT	81
ODE ON THE BOSS	82
ODE ON A GALLANT PHILOSOPHER	83
ODE ON THE UNIVERSAL RELATION	84
ODE ON THE YOUTH	85
ODE ON THE DOWNTRODDEN	86
ODE ON THE DIVINE LOVE OF A MOTHER	87

ODE ON THE SOBBING HEART 89
ODE ON THE DARK DEMON 90
ODE ON SLEEP 91
ODE ON THE DIVERSITY 92
ODE ON AN AUTOCRAT 93
ODE ON THE SNUFF 94
ODE ON A TEA-CUP 95
ODE ON THE ANTS 96
ODE ON THE LEISURE 97
ODE ON HARMONY 98
ODE ON THE GREATEST ARTIST 99
ODE ON A TRAIN 100
ODE ON A LAMENTED BUTTERFLY 102
ODE ON THE AUTOBIOGRAPHY OF AN UMBRELLA 104
ODE ON THE WILD ANIMALS 105
ODE ON THE UNPRIVILEGED 106
ODE ON A NEGLECTED CANDLESTICK 107
ODE ON THE SINKING SHIP 108
ODE ON THE CHURCH BELL... 109
ODE ON THE CHRISTMAS DAY 110
ODE ON THE BEAUTY OF DARKNESS 111
ODE ON DREAMS... 112
ODE ON PATRIOTISM 113

ODE ON DEATH	115
ODE ON A FRIEND IN NEED	116
ODE ON THE ECHOING GREEN	118
ODE ON THE TEMPTATION	119
ODE ON THE NURSING MOTHER	120
ODE ON THE SWEET LADY	121
ODE ON THE LITTLE	122
ODE ON THE SOUL	124
ODE ON HIS KINDNESS	125
ODE ON RELIGION	127
ODE ON A FOSTER CHILD	129
ODE ON THE NATURE	130
ODE ON THE RAIN	132
ODE ON THE FEIGNED LOVER	134
ODE ON THE DEEP SEA	135
ODE ON THE SWAN-SONG	136
ODE ON A STREET BEGGAR	137
ODE ON THE SINCERE SERVICE	139
ODE ON THE TRAGEDY	140
ODE ON THE GOALLESS LIFE	141
ODE ON THE DEJECTED LOVER	142
ODE ON THE IMAGINATION	143
ODE ON THE DEPARTED FATHER	144

ODE ON THE VISION OF LIFE	145
ODE ON THE PREPARATION FOR DEATH	146
ODE ON THE DEPARTED SOUL	147
ODE ON THE STRUGGLE OF LIFE	149
ODE ON THE KINDNESS	150
ODE ON THE UNIVERSAL BROTHERHOOD	151
ODE ON THE EQUILIBRIUM	152
ODE ON THE MUSIC OF WORDS	153
ODE ON THE CREATION OF THE UNIVERSE	155
ODE ON THE WAYFARER	156
ODE ON THE DOOMS DAY	157
ODE ON A BIRD OF BEAUTY	158
ODE ON THE WINGED WORLD	160
ODE ON THE RHYTHMS	161
ODE ON THE VIRGIN FLOWER	163
ODE ON THE METEORIC RISE OF A POLITICIAN	164
ODE ON A SOBBING DEER	165
ODE ON THE INGREDIENTS OF LIFE	166
ODE ON THE UPS AND DOWNS OF LIFE	167
ODE ON THE ABANDONED CHILD	168
ODE ON THE BEAUTY OF THE LAKE	169
ODE ON THE HAVE-NOTS	170
ODE ON THE POSTHUMOUS CHILD	171

ODE ON MISS BEAUTY	172
ODE ON THE BODY AND MIND	173
ODE ON OLD AGE	174
ODE ON THE BIRTHDAY CELEBRATION	175
ODE ON WEAL AND WOE	176
ODE ON HUMBLE PRAYER TO GOD	177
ODE ON TRUTH AND BEAUTY	178
ODE ON THE JUDGMENT OF THE PEACOCK THE GREAT	179
ODE ON THE MERRIMENT	180
ODE ON FREEDOM OF INDIA	181
ODE ON AN ACT OF KINDNESS	182
ODE ON 'FOOD'	183
ODE ON THE VILLAGE AND TOWN	184
ODE ON A PEN	185
ODE ON THE HERMITAGE	186
ODE ON THE VIRGIN FLOWER	187
ODE ON THE FLOOD	188
ODE ON THE BEAUTY OF DARKNESS	189
ODE ON THE MONKEY MIND	190
ODE ON CO-OPERATION	191
THE EPILOGUE	192

ODE TO THE GREEN LADY

I happened to see, the beautiful green lady;
Full to the brim of her youth.
Just like a lily in bloom
In a showery afternoon.
I never expected her in such a lonely bower
And in such an ecstatic mood.
I could nothing but wonder
When I saw her unique beauty.
My heart danced with joy
In the solitary greenery.

She was clad in green attire,
In conformity with her tender age.
And her sweet voice enchanted me
Like that of a nightingale.

She was singing and dancing to herself,
Just like a country girl;
Nodding her head at every step
With the whistling sound of the air.

She arrested my attention to her
In such an overwhelming manner;
That I remained spellbound
With the magic of her melodious sound.

I looked at her with motionless eyes
To enjoy her unique beauty.
She observed it and said,
"Why are you looking at me?"

I woke up from my dreamy state and said,
"I am drinking your beauty to the lees,
Thinking it a heavenly bliss."
As your beauty enchanted my eyes.

She smiled and said with a sigh!
"It is a momentary thing to the masculine being
To love and forget the opposite sex
In the twinkling of an eye."

I was so impressed with her melodious voice
That I could not utter any word.
As I was totally overpowered by her
Just like a hungry bee on the blooming flower.

ODE ON CHARACTER

Character is the crown and glory of life.
Without it, a man is no better than a beast.
And appears ignominious to the society,
Just like an uncrowned king.

A life without morality, loses its humidity;
And cannot be flourished.
Just like a little plant cannot be developed
If it is not properly nourished.

A life without character loses its glamour.
And becomes drudgery and dull;
Without affording any pleasure -
Just like a faded flower.

It makes our life bright and beautiful
With the constant charming touch.
As the sky becomes bright and cloudless
With the sweet touch of the rising sun.

It acts as the recording machine of our activities.
And records them like a computer -
From our very birth on the Earth
To our eternal departure.

Character is the inherent quality of a man
Which helps him to win the battle of life -
Defeating all sorts of adversities;
That beset its smooth sailing.

It acts as the beacon light
Through which we see the path of life.
And reached at the destination
Avoiding all sorts of humiliations.

A man of character wins the heart of the people
Through his amiable disposition.
And is held high in the minds of men
With due respects and devotion.

Character is the mirror of our life,
Through which our life is truly reflected.
And we see everything far behind,
With the help of this magic casement.

Character is the 'KOHINOOR' of human life, -
Which distinguishes itself from the other;
For its everlasting brightness
And overwhelming power.

A man of no character, on the other hand;
Is just like a vessel without any Rudder,
Which floats all over the ocean;
But cannot reach at the destination.

ODE ON THE DEVOTED LOVERS

I have five devoted lovers of my own-
The summer, the winter, the rains, the spring and the autumn.
All of them love me very much,
And I live with them in close touch.
They cannot bear my separation,
Just like Romeo and Juliet;
Who have been made for each other
And termed as classical lovers.

They live with me throughout the year,
And come one after another
To serve me like a devoted lover
Removing all sorts of barriers.
Only to replenish my heart with cheers.

The summer serves me with sweet fruits
When I am fatigued with the Sun.
And redress my weariness
By waving the natural fan.

The winter gives me comforts,
By supplying winter clothes.
And serves me palatable dishes;
Containing tasteful vegetables.
She warms me up through sunshine,
And we embrace each other like husband and wife.

The rains turns the environment silvery white
And keeps it free from pollution;
Making a healthy atmosphere,

For the new habitation.

The autumn appears before me
With her lovely sight.
And my heart dances with joy
When I enjoy the moonlit night.

The spring turns the surroundings green-
And the people called her the queen of flowers.
The cuckoo sings sweetly in the bowers
To fill the grieved heart with pleasure.
My pensive attitude turns into jocund mood.
And I think, I am enjoying the green childhood;
With my play-mates in the green ground.
And I see beauty in everything,
Even in the meanest beings.

None can imagine
What an enjoyable life I lead!
With my devoted lovers
In the beautiful surroundings.

But the irony of fate dragged me down,
From the heaven to the hell.
And makes my life miserable
When the spring divorced me like a pale flower without scent.

ODE ON THE DESERT

People call me the king of the deserts,
As they think I have no heart.
And compare me with shylock the Jew
Considering my outward view.

My heart consists of barren sands,
Where there is no place for fertile lands-
For the flowering bower of the bees.
And to entertain the weary travelers of the oasis.

But alas! Will anyone tell
Who has made me so cruel?
Banishing far away from the habitation
And dragging me down such a plight condition.

I have a kind heart of my own,
Which is not visible to anyone.
Just like the Falgu river
That flows throughout the inner.

I shed tears a lot at night
When I find none by my side.
To console my anguished heart
With a soothing touch of a lover.

ODE ON A LOVELESS LIFE

Love and let love is the very foundation of life.
Without it, the life cannot be flourished;
At its proper form and feature,
And looks very ugly and tastes bitter.

A loveless life is a current less river;
Which cannot flow on its course
Being surrounded my deep moss.
And looks like a dead one.
Though there is plenty of water.

Current connects one river to another,
And flows towards the sea;
Where lies the ultimate goal.
Love greets one heart to another,
And follows towards the universality;
Which binds the world into an undivided whole.

As we cannot think of a river without the current.
So we cannot think about a life without love inherent.
A current less river is no river in anyway.
And a loveless life is no life, so to say.

Current makes a river alive
And helps it to flow on its course.
Love makes a life flavorus to us
Sweeping away the fetidness at source.

Love is life, life is love;
Both of them are the two sides of a same coin.
And we cannot distinguish them by their outer differences;
As they are indivisible one.

ODE ON THE DESIRE

None is immortal in this mortal world,
From the ignoble animal to man.
All are in the cruel hands of Death
And meet the same fate.

We come and go like a magic show;
Shown by the great Magician.
Who regulates the world after His own intension,
From the very beginning of the creation.

He cares a little for our passions,
And acts on His own desires;
Without considering that of us
Who are living in this universe.

We are to be very serious
To materialize our desires.
Just like the farmers who cultivate the land
And grow corn with deep devotion.

From the very beginning of sowing seeds
To the end of harvesting the same.
They spend many a sleepless night
For solving the various problems.

'No pain, No gain' -
There goes the famous proverb.
We are to struggle hard,
If we wish to fulfill our desires.

ODE ON THE NOBLE HERITAGE

From the days of yore,
India has a noble heritage of her own;
To live and let live -
And not to live alone.

All men and women are brothers and sisters
Living in the same family;
Forgetting the racial differences
Of the ignoble caste and creed.
And leading a life of great harmony
Throughout the eternity.

Universal brotherhood
Was their code of conduct.
And they love each other
Like own brother and sister.

The motherly feeling arouse in her
When she was conquered by the foreigners.
And looked upon them as own sons and daughters
As she looked upon to those of the Indians.

The foreigners turned into Indians
Forgetting their foreign entity.
And live together as brothers and sisters
For the deep love and of divine dignity.

We are proud of the noble Heritage
And bow down our head to show respect.
All our differences disappeared;
When we called ourselves Indians.

The word Indian is an enchanted word,
Which binds all of us together.
And inspires to lead a harmonious life.
Just like that of a conjugal lover -
Form by the unknown husband and wife.

ODE ON DUTY

What to do and what not to do
Will be decided by you,
As you are the authority -
To mould your life as you like.

The world is full of virtue and vice,
Served before you in a wide dish.
You are to take from it;
Either the bitter virtue or the delicious vice.

The delicious vice will attract you more
For its apparent smell and taste.
But it will lead you to the hell
Where resides permanent Pain.

The bitter virtue, on the other hand;
Has no charm of its own.
But it will lead you to Heaven
And make your life a fruitful one.

ODE ON POVERTY

Poverty, my bosom friend;
I bow down my head with reverence.
As you have showed me the path of truth,
Through which I achieved the goal of life;
In a fierce fight with the Misfortune.
Which besets my life from the very childhood.

When I fell in deep distress,
None came for my help.
But you remained by my side,
Like an unfailing friend.

You saved me from the agonies of life,
Which crippled my body and mind;
Covering my hopes so high,
Just like the cloud in the sky.

Your sincere love and devotion
Rejuvenated me with hopes and aspirations.
And inspired me to win the battle of life
Defeating the enemies in a fierce fight.

Everyone fights shy of you
For your ugly appearance
But I love and adore you
As my beloved friend.

You have guided me towards the goal of life,
Just like the engine of a Train.
And I reached at the destination

With your sincere love and help.

You have inspired me with deep dedication
To fight against all sorts of social oppressions;
Which crippled the Nation stopping its motion
Leaving it into a plight condition.

I bow to thee, my sweetest friend;
As you have enkindled my imagination by thy fire,
To achieve the goal of life with my lyre;
Penetrating through the debris of dark despair.

ODE ON A LIFE LONG PRISONER

I am a lifelong Prisoner,
In the prison-house of the world.
Where People live together,
Forgetting their own abode.

The world is a tourist lodge
We come here as the travelers.
And to leave the Lodge
When the tour is over.

None of us permanent here.
And none has any permanent claim,
Over the wealth and riches of the world;
For which we are struggling in vain.

Everyone is born to die,
And we have to die one day or another;
Leaving behind us the wealth and riches
For which we are hankering after.

Our life is limited by time,
 But duty knows no limit.
We are to finish the duty at our disposal
Within the framework of the life.

If we neglect to do our duty in time,
The duty will never be finished.
We will be held responsible
And will surely be punished.

Our benevolent Father leads us

Towards the path of justice.
And encourages us at every step
Not to compromise with injustice.

If we follow His dictum,
From the very beginning of the life;
The life will be flourished to the brim
Just like a hilly Stream.

If we fail to follow him,
The life will lose its charms.
And we cannot enjoy the life
In the true sense of the term.

ODE ON AN UNKNOWN BOATMAN

I am to go many a mile before the sunset,
Otherwise, my journey will be hampered,
And I may not step any further
Due to widespread darkness.

I have to cross a forest and a river,
Within the time at my disposal.
I quickened my pace like a galloping horse
To reach at the destination on the appointed hour.

I was breathing fast to fast my journey.
As the sun was descending quickly;
Covering the earth like a sword in the sheath
How can I cross the river and the bridge?

I left no stone unturned to cross the river.
But all my attempts were in vain.
And I left alone in the dark forest.
With a quivering heart for the rest.

At the dead of night, I saw a vision;
Who propelled me towards the river.
Where I saw a boatman awaiting
To lead me towards the destination.

As soon as I reached the other bank,
I found no trace of the boatman;
Who helped me to cross the river
Just like a selfless lover.

My eyes were glistening white,

When I missed my friend with me;
Who helped me in my journey
In the midst of shrouded agony.

ODE ON A FLOWERY BOWER

I wander lonely as a vagabond.
Suddenly, I saw a bunch of flowers;
Singing and dancing in the bower,
With the gentle breeze as the partner.

They captured my attention in such a manner
That I remained spellbound.
And could not utter any word
Just like the hypnotized one.

I gazed at them with romantic eyes.
And could not express my feeling in wonder
As I am totally over powered
With the inexpressible joy at the hour.

They were dancing with melodious song
Which I could not understand at all.
But it sounded very sweet to me
And leaves a lasting impression in my memory.

I was so overwhelmed with the song
That I never forget it in my life.
As it gives me pleasure in the solitary hour
When I left alone in the bower.

A thing of beauty is a joy forever.
And a sweet memory can never fade away.
It remains intact in the casket of our memory.
And gives pleasure at the time of melancholy.

ODE ON THE HAPPINESS

We want happiness at every step
Without sorrows and sufferings.
But happiness is a bird of wings
And is out of our reach.

Our hankering soars very high
To catch the bird in the sky.
And to enjoy its charming beauty
With all its divine dignity.

But it is hard to catch the bird,
As it soars very high in the sky.
And disappears like a golden deer,
Leaving us in the debris of dark despair.

We cannot move a single step,
Without the sweet touch of happiness.
And think our life is of no use
Just like a fused tube.

Happiness is a relative term
And varies from man to man.
What is happiness to one,
May be sufferings to the other.

It also depends on the state of mind,
What is happiness to me now,
May be sufferings after sometime.
As it has no permanent appeal.

Life is a strange mixture of the weal and woe.
Both of them are intermingled;
And cannot be separated from each other
As they are inseparable ingredients.

We should not run after happiness
As, it is not the goal of life.
We are to drink the life to the lees
To enjoy the life with its varied tastes.

ODE TO THE MOTHERLAND

I have been banished from my motherland
Where I first open my eyes.
She loved me as dearly
As mother loves her child.

She gave me bread
To maintain my health.
And quenched my thirst
With the milk of her breast.

She provided me shelter
When I became very tired.
And could not move any further
Being fatigued with the Sun.

When I feel ill and confined to bed,
She nursed me day and night.
And gave comfort to my anguished heart,
With her sincere motherly nursing.

She saved me from the jaws of Death,
Even at the cost of her life.
I shall remain ever grateful to her,
And her selfless sacrifice.

As ill luck would have it –
The cursed partition has driven me far away,
Where I have been residing with the step mother;
Without any care and affection.

Being deprived of her affection,
I am leading here a hazardous life;
Full of sorrows and sufferings.
Just like an abandoned child.

ODE ON BEAUTY

Beauty is to see, not to touch;-
There goes the proud proverb.
If we touch it now and then;
The beauty losses it purity,
And will no longer be charming to us
Just like a faded flower.

A thing of beauty is a source of eternal joy
And makes our life enjoyable.
Leaving aside the impurities of life
It makes the life viable.

It is the unique creation of the Almighty,
Which refreshes our mind banishing sorrows and sufferings.
And inspires us to overcome the distress,
Just like a bosom friend.

We love those beautiful things
Which enchanted our eyes.
And help us to lead a pleasant life.
Forgetting the ugliness of sorrows and sufferings.

A thing of beauty knows to death.
And remains always afresh.
Even in the midst of sorrows and sufferings,
It finds out the goal of life.

An ugly thing, on the other hand; has no charm of its own.

And vitiates our mind and gives no comfort.
Just like an evil company, it leads us towards the hell,
Deviating from the path of truth and happiness.

ODE TO THE APRIL SUN

Oh! My beloved April Sun,
Exert your Heat as far as you can.
Your Heat is not so unkind
As the ingratitude of a man.

Your Heat burns only our body,
Which can easily be cured;
By applying medicine to the injured.
But man's ingratitude is a separate thing
And it burns both body and mind at the same time,
Which cannot be cured with any medicine.
It constantly burns till our death.
Like a criminal of life long imprisonment.

I welcome thee, my bosom friend;
To exert your Heat mercilessly on me,
In order to forget those ungrateful beings
Who feigned themselves to be my best friends.
And left no stone unturned for doing me harm,
In their heinous disguise of the well-wishers.

ODE ON THE FEIGNING FRIENDSHIP

We have come alone in this world,
And we are to depart alone from it.
Leaving everything far behind;-
Our children and belongings.

Why should we try so hard
To bind ourselves with relations?
Which is nothing but a fruitless effort,
And has no practical implications.

When we fall in deep distress,
We gather the bitter experience;
From our feigning friends and relatives
Who are of no practical use
Just like that of a fused tube.

When we breathe our last,
None will follow us;
As a token of love and sympathy
Which we cherished so long.

They will forget our prolonged friendship.
After our departure from the Earth.
And paid no homage to our memory
Which looks like a comical farce.

ODE TO THE BELOVED 'SHE'

I hail to thee, my beloved 'She';
Please come and embrace me –
To extinguish the 'Fire of Bereavement';
Which burns my body and mind always.
Just like the poison of a snake.

One may get rid of the pain from poison
By administrating medicine.
But none can get rid of the pain
Infused through thy Sting.

Everyone is bound to accept Thee;
Sooner or later.
As it is the ultimate goal of all;
Who are in this mortal world.

Thy constant kiss will help me to reach
At the ultimate goal of my life.
Where resides my beloved she;
Awaiting eagerly for me.

ODE ON THE MILLENNIUM

Come! Come! Come!
The bounteous Millennium;
To illuminate the world
By your natural grace and fervour
To rescue us from the Den of the Sufferings –
A legacy left by your elder sisters; -
The fugitive 'Ninety-nine'.

Come and Embrace us with the motherly affection
To bind the people of the world into a single nation.
Forgetting the charms of plurality
Which drives the world towards Futility.

Come, our beloved Millennium!
Crossing the threshold of the New Year;
To save the world from imminent danger
As an affectionate saviour.

Please sweep away the corruptions,
With your deep love and devotion;
In order to create a congenial atmosphere
In establishing Peace and Prosperity
For the future generation of the humanity.

ODE ON A SAD BEREAVEMENT

We cannot forget the hijackers
Who hijacked the plane to Kandahar.
And created a lot of agonies
To the innocent passengers.

They were deprived of food and drink
As it was the hijacker's decree;-
To go without food and drink
As long as their demands fulfilled.

We can never forget Rupin's tragic death,
Who went to Nepal to enjoy the charms of life;
With Rachana, his newly married wife.
But he never came back to his residence
As he faced the dire consequence.

What a tragedy lies with Rachana,
Who will have to lead a Rudderless life;
Throughout the turbulent ocean of the world
Without any proper guide.

Can anyone tell who will be held responsible?
For inflicting catastrophe;
At the very outset of Rachana's life?

ODE ON LOVE

Love associated with Passion
Is no love in the true sense of the term;
Which intensifies hankering
And makes the life drudgery and dull.

It has a characteristic of its own
To give something to get something more.
When it fails to get something in exchange of giving
The real trouble then begins.

The true love is selfless in nature.
And displays a different character.
Which knows no condition to serve
Like that of the former.

It comes from the heaven and flows over the world;
Sweeping away the impurities of Heart
Just like that of the Ganges water.

It serves as the Beacon light
Which removes the darkness of mind.
And guides the soul to achieve the goal.
In the midst of sorrows and sufferings.

It comes from the heaven
With motherly love and charity;
To rescue the malicious world
From the jaws of the Brutality.

It joins the broken fragment of the heart together
Just like a strong adhesive.

And helps us to lead a harmonious life
With fellow neighbourly feelings.

ODE ON THE BLACK CURTAIN

All the world is a stage.
And all of us are players.
We are to exhibit ourselves on the stage,
Just like actors and actresses.

Our life is divided into various scenes,
Just like the scenes of a drama.
We are to display the activities of life
Through the life's Panorama.

Our very birth is the entrance on the stage,
And the death signifies the exit.
We are to show the scenes of life,
Within our life-time.

From our very birth to the earth,
The play starts on the stage.
And the different characters play their roles
From the beginning to the end.

If we perform well on the stage,
We will be greeted by the audience.
But if we fail to do it properly,
We must be condemned by them.

Everything depends on the performance.
If the drama ends in a tragic way,
We must call it a tragedy.
And if ends in a happy reunion,
It may aptly be called a Comedy.

In this way, we perform our roles;
As actors and actresses.
And bid goodbye from the stage,
When falls the 'Black Curtain'.

ODE ON TIME

Time and tide wait for none.
Both of them run apace,
Towards the destination;
Like a galloping horse.

Life is nothing but some total of time.
Without proper use of time
The life cannot be prosperous.
Just like that of a regulator.

As the regulator regulates the machine,
And helps it to work smoothly.
So the time regulates our life
To work harmoniously to the path of destiny.

If we use every moment of our life properly
The life will be flourished to the fullest extent.
And will be the source of enjoyment –
From the beginning to the end.

If we do not give it due importance,
The life will lose its fragrance.
And will no longer be charming to us,
Just like a river besetting with the moss-
Cannot reach at the destination.

ODE ON THE SOLITARY LOVER

   I fell in love with one of her six daughters,
Who was full to the brim of her youth.
She attracted my attention to her
As she looked very beautiful.

Her eyes were black in color,
And hair with many a curl.
Her teeth were glistening white,
Just like white pearls.

Her face was oval in shape,
And the body was rosy in color.
She appeared before me,
Just like a blooming flower.

She was clad in green,
Inconformity with her age.
And she looked so charming
That even the sage would be tempted.

I met her in a solitary bower.
She was dancing like a mirthful flower.
I looked at her forgetting my entity,
As she was an epitome of beauty.

What a beauty she possessed!
None can express it in language.
I looked at her with motionless eyes,
Just like a mad lover in disguise.

She observed it and beckoned me

With a silvery smile to her.
I responded instantly to her magic call,
Just like a Bee on the call of a flower.

We expressed our heart within ourselves
As it was a very solitary place.
Our love overflowed the bower like the current of the river.
And both of us turned into ideal lover.

ODE ON THE PSALM OF LIFE

I am at the fag-end of my life
And hear the clarion call,
To go back to my own abode,
Where I have left my all.

But yet I have to do a lot of works
For the people around me.
Who have been deprived of everything.
And lead a very miserable life.

They have been robbed of the amenities
Which make the life, a pleasant one.
By the pirate leaders of the day
Who feigned themselves their all.

But, in fact, they are vampire bats.
Always sucking blood from the hearts.
And turned them out of the existence;
When they think them of no use.
Just like sugarcane after sucking juice.

I am to blossom just like a flower,
In order to cherish those hearts;
Who never enjoyed the bliss of life
And struggling hard to survive.

ODE ON A NEGLECTED FLOWER

I am a neglected nameless flower,
Bloomed in the garden of God;
Without care and nourishment
To the surprise of all.

None show me any sympathy
And give me any food;
Which my cousins have received,
From their very childhood.

I have been banished in this lonely place,
And none looks after me.
Just like Robinson Crusoe
Who was living alone by the sea.

I am struggling hard for my existence,
Like my poor brethren;
Who are being trampled under foot
By the Dictators every now and then.

Yet I think my life will be fruitful;
If I can afford cheers to them.
Who never witnessed it,
During the whole course of their life.

ODE ON LUCY

Lucy, Lucy, my dear Lucy;
You are very diligent and badly busy.
And served the Gods and Goddesses of the Heaven
Like a devoted servant.

You have been driven
From the region of Heaven;
For neglecting your duty.
Just like the Goddess of the Mythology.

You have been banished from the Heaven
By the Heavenly Gods and Goddesses.
For rigorous imprisonment in this world;
As per committed crimes
During a certain period of time.

Your imprisonment has been cut short,
For your sincere work;
Which moved the judge and set you free
From the imprisonment by His decree.

You left the world and went to your own abode
Leaving all of us here.
Though we are awaiting for you
Through shedding tears.

ODE ON THE UNIVERSAL FRATERNITY

God loves them best,
Who love their fellow beings;
As brothers and sisters
Of the same family.

We are to work together
To maintain the world's prosperity.
Just like the members of the joint family.
Who works for its integrity.

What He demands from us
Is unquestioning faith in Him.
And the deep devotion without condition
To serve the oppressed humanity.

If we serve the people around us
At the time of the danger.
They will bow down their heads with reverence
And will be turned into our harbingers.

If we think the world, our family;
And the people our brothers and sisters.
Our abodes will turned into Heaven
And He will be our universal Father.

There will be no distinction between man and man,
All of us will be the same rank.
And the universal fraternity will be established
Which is the precondition of world peace.

ODE ON THE DEATHLESS LIFE

Man is born to die,
None can avoid it.
As it is the universal verdict
Announced by the Almighty.

Our life is just like the water of the Petal,
It may fall down at anytime;
Without giving any notice to us
As it is predestined.

Death is our best friend,
And guides us as a Rudder.
Which shows the passage of our life,
And instructs us to fulfil our desire;
Within the time at our disposal.

Our life will be useless,
If there is no death.
As it increases the flavour of our life,
Just like the tasty spice.

A rudderless ship cannot find its way
In the turbulent ocean.
A deathless life cannot reach as its coveted destination.

ODE ON POLLUTION

We are living in the age of pollution –
There goes the slogan.
Everything is polluted here;-
Water, environment and the air.

Nothing can be found here fresh;
Even the mother's breast;
Which is so essential
For the child's development.

If the creation goes on pollution
In such a rapid way.
The civilization will come to an end
And the romance will wither away.

We are to take active step
To avert the pollution.
With a view to saving the humanity
As well as the whole of creation.

If we do not avert it actively,
It will spread its empire
Just like an imperialist.
Who knows no limit of his desire.

The pollution Demon will defeat us
In the battle of pollution.
And sentenced to death by suffocation;
As we are vanquished by the Demon.

ODE ON THE NIGHT QUEEN

I am Miss Night Queen,
I open my eyes at night.
People called me white lady,
As my body is milky white.

My fans robbed me off
From my mother's lap;
When she was in noonday dreams.
 I was at a loss and screamed.

I began to weep bitterly,
When I did not find my mother.
They consoled me again and again
As they were my well-wishers.

I longed to get back my mother's lap,
Where I have been born and brought up.
They remained silent for a little while
And threatened to tear me off.

They enjoyed me at their sweet will
Kissing all over my body.
And thrown me away on the dust
As it is their usual hobby.

None showed me any sympathy.
And enjoyed my beauty.
I remain neglected on the dust.
Just like a virgin after molestation.

ODE ON WATER

Water is life and life is water.
Both of them are co-related with each other.
We cannot expect one's existence
Leaving out the other into consideration.

They are like the twin brothers,
If one is attacked by the infectious disease;
The other will automatically be attacked by the same.
Just think, the curious relation between them.

We may live without food
For certain period of time.
But cannot live without water
For a pretty while.

Water is as precious as our life.
We are to keep it pure from pollution.
If water is polluted, life will be polluted;
And the civilization will come to an end.

Water is our beloved mother.
And serves us round the clock.
Rendering her valuable service
In some form or other.

It sweeps away the road
Just like a sweeper.
And keeps away from the microbes
Which are the root of infectious fever.

What a selfless service it renders to us,
From the very beginning to the end!
None can believe it in this world
As it is really unbelievable.
As we cannot expect our existence
Without the beloved mother.
So we cannot expect our life
Without pure water.

ODE ON OLD MONKEY

Once I came across a group of monkeys,
Assembled together under a banyan tree.
They were singing and dancing in their own way,
To enjoy the bliss of a carefree life.

I halted there for sometime
To enjoy their carefree life.
As I was in pensive mood
And nothing to do to pass away the time.

I saw an old monkey sitting on the branch of a tree;
And gave a unique verdict to be followed
By his fellow brethren;
Who were sitting underneath.

He told to follow the norms of life
To keep the environment free from pollution.
And to save the life of the future generation
From the hands of the utter destruction.

He gave the requisite instructions to the followers
How to keep the environment free from pollution.
They gave a serious thought to it.
By publishing a manuscript.
And handed over the same
To the related departments.

They wrote in the footnote –
A warning to one and all;
To keep the environment free from pollution
Within seven days to come.

If anyone failed to obey the notice
He will be severely punished.
And this punishment even be raised
Up to the death sentence.

The notice was first served to the Mayor
Who is the head of the local body.
His duty is to see the interest of the people
As he is the people's representative.

After receiving the notice
The Mayor burst into laugh.
And paid no heed to it.
As it has been served by the beast.

After seven days of the notice
The monkeys entered into the Mayor's office.
And killed the Mayor then and there
When he was going to fire.

The mayor learnt the proper lesson
At the cost of his life;
And inspired the people around
To keep the environment sound.

ODE ON MRS. WHITE

People called me Mrs. White
But my origin is red.
I appeared white before you
When I come out from the mother's breast.

People called me balanced diet.
And prefer me best.
So they serve me to their sweet Hearts
And reserved for the guests.

I feed my own children
As well as those of the others.
Without taking any discrimination
Just like a devoted mother.

The doctors prescribed me for those
Who have little hope to regain.
I nursed them round the clock
To rejuvenate them to life again.

But alas! My quality is changed now and then
And I become thinner to thinner.
For the free mixing with the step mother
When I was put into the same container.

This is not all, they change my form;
 From the liquidity to the solid one.
In order to profit much more
Ignoring the demand of the poor.

As a result, the poor suffers from anaemia

Without proper nourishment.
And lead a shorter life
What a tragic bereavement!

ODE ON THE MEMORIAL

You are not a tomb but a temple of love,
Erected by the great lover.
In order to pay due homage to the beloved
After the eternal departure.

You have been erected
In the days of yore.
Yet you look very lovely
As lovely as before.

No blemish can erase your beauty,
As you are the embodiment of love.
And love remains love always,
As it is unblemished in character.

You are one of the Seven Wonders of the World.
And people thronged around you.
Just like a swarm of bees on the flowers,
To enjoy the wonders in view.

You are the eternal source of inspiration,
And inspire us in every walk of life.
When we are depressed by the surroundings,
And find no way to survive.

You are running towards the Eternity
Cherishing the lofty idea of love.
"Love is Heaven, Heaven is love" –
That is all we know on the earth
And yet to know in the long run.

ODE ON THE GUIDING SPIRIT

I may not get any touch from you,
As you are far away from me.
But I feel your active participation
In every walk of my life.

Your memory acts as a cellular phone,
And give me the requisite information.
I am guided by them at every step,
When I face any hesitation.

None can see you,
As you are invisible.
But I can see and hear you
Just like the things visible.

You are guiding me
Just like a pole star.
And I am being guided by you,
As you are my well-wisher.

All my hopes are to be nipped in the bud,
If you do not show me the path.
And help me to reach at the goal of my life,
I should have to shed tears all the while.

ODE ON THE GREAT GRANDMOTHER

My dear great grandmother,
You are giving us shelter;
From the beginning of the civilization.
Just like the beloved mother.

You are protecting us from the heat and rain
Giving enthusiasm to work again;
When we are fatigued with the sun
And cannot work any further.

Your healing touch makes us fresh.
And we resume our duty again.
Being rejuvenated by you
With your profound love and attachment.

We are doing our duty
Forgetting the weariness of life.
As nobody can achieve happiness
Without sorrows and sufferings.

You have taught us a great lesson
Weal and woe are woven fine.
And we are to accept both of them at the same time
As they are pre-destined.

ODE ON THE NEWBORN BABY

You are the embodiment of love and beauty.
And descended from the Heaven with a promise;
To serve the oppressed humanity
With deep love and divine Piety.

We are awaiting for you year after year
To welcome you with joyful tears.
For saving the world from the hands of cruelty.
Which has banished the morality.

The world has turned into the den of beasts
And people run after their own interest
Ignoring the interest of others.
Just like that of a butcher.

You should come with the divine message
To serve the humanity with selfless interest.
Removing the distinction between man and man.
As all of them belong to same origin.

You will turn the malicious world
Into the pleasant paradise.
People think for each other,
And the world will be free from malice.

When the people will be united together
Sacrificing their selfish nature.
The world will evolve into a mighty nation
Forgetting the racial discrimination.

ODE ON THE RETURN JOURNEY

My journey has come to an end,
As I reached at the fag-end;
And will have to return Home,
To the anxious Father of my own.

He is waiting for me year after year,
As I have left Him there.
Without any communication between us
Which made Him anxious.

I have forgotten the Father
Who sends me here;
With some definite aims in view.
But I failed and left them due,
Living amidst the pleasures of life.
Just like a bee in the hive.

My Father may be angry with me
For neglecting my duty.
And may not allow me to enter the Room
Where shall I go and how to bloom?

I have nothing but to shed tears
Sitting on the street like an orphan.
And none come to show me sympathy,
As I am detracted from the path of life.

Being detached from all,
I heard the clarion call;
Listen my child "You are rectified".

I welcome you to live with me in the heavenly paradise.

My heart overflows its banks,
When I heard the clarion call.
My life blossomed into a flower
And emits fragrance all over.

ODE ON THE BOSOM FRIEND

I come from the Heaven,
Just like the drops of kindness;
To serve the oppressed Humanity
With the divine love and dignity.

People called me their bosom friend;
As I serve them all the while.
And they cannot expect their existence
Without my proper sacrifice.

I am favourite to the poor.
As I sustained their life
With the milk of my breast;
When they find no place to rest.
And wander hither and thither
In search of food and shelter.

I serve the poor of the world,
As their devoted mother.
When I give them my cold breast
During the heated summer.

Someone called me the Pious lady.
As I wash away the impurities,
And make the world free from pollution
With my deep love and devotion.

I am near and dear to the people so much
That they give their new-born baby my sweet touch.
And give the same touch to them
Who are awaiting for death.

ODE ON THE CREATIVITY OF LIFE

Life is not a pleasure garden
But a garden; full of thorns.
We are to labour hard
If we wish to pluck flowers.

"None but the brave deserves the fair" –
There goes the proud proverb.
We are to fight tooth and nail
To maintain our existence.

The defeated has no place,
But to succumb to death;
And leads a miserable life
Without rendering any sacrifice.

The winner, on the other hand;
Drink the life to the lees.
And makes the life pleasurable
In the midst of sorrows and sufferings.

An idle brain is the devils workshop.
As it has no creativity of its own.
And looks like a current less river,
Surrounded by the deep moss.

A currentless river cannot flow on its course,
Losing its power of motion.
And remains stagnant all the while,
Being detached from the ocean.

ODE ON PEACE

Peace is the very basis of our life.
Without peace, the life cannot be viable.
And looks drudgery and dull
Just like a tree without flowers.

It is like the current of the river
The current makes the river viable
And leads it towards the seashore,
Where lies its ultimate goal.

Peace is a strange mixture of weal and woe.
None can receive only the weal
Leaving out the woe far behind.
As both of them run hand in hand
Just like two bosom friends.

We are to accept both of them
To enjoy the variety of life.
Without variety, life loses its charms
 And appears before us like a boredom.

ODE ON WAR

War is the worst curse of our life.
It occurs due to selfishness of mankind.
A selfish man always thinks for his self-interest,
And does not allow anyone to run with him a race.
Where lies the seeds of war –
Which is the curse of all disasters.

It is just like a sharpen blade;
Which can only cut and bleed.
But cannot afford any relief;
To the winner or the vanquished.

Yet we undergo such a shameful war,
To prove our superiority over the other;
Through this mischievous way
What a kingly gesture does it display!

War brings immeasurable miseries
To our peaceful life.
It kills the husband leaving his wife.
And vanishes the mother keeping her child.
Can anyone imagine
What a plight legacy it leaves behind?

The widows cry for their husbands,
The husbands for the wives.
The mother cries for her son
And the father for the total annihilation.

It can, in no way, be a path to peace;
As it pollutes everything.

It brings disaster to our normal life.
Where there is no place of love and sympathy.
Which binds all of us together.
And leads us to the path of integrity.

War is our malicious friend
As it gives us no benefit.
So we are to fight against it.
With all our might and main.

ODE TO THE SELFISH MAN

Hello! Mr. Selfish man,
Why do you ignore your fan?
Please peep a deep at us
As we are your admirers.

We are living here
In the midst of dust and rain;
Without any shade over our head,
To protect us from sunshine and rain.

You are living under the roof of a house.
And enjoying the amenities of life.
But we are being deprived of it,
Please tell, on what right?

Our mother may be different,
But Father is the same.
We have equal rights to enjoy
The prevailing privilege.

You have prevented us
To enjoy the bliss of life.
But we are sacrificing ourselves
To make your life bright.

We are refreshing your heart,
Just like a girlfriend
And make your life viable
Through giving our sweet enjoyment.

But alas! You do not think a little for us;

And make our life miserable.
As you do not give us the due share
For making our life enjoyable.

Do you think what would be happened
When we will no longer be in the world?
Who will cherish your heart in distress
And give you comfort like a girl friend?

ODE ON THE CAGED LIFE

I am a caged man
Living under your supervision.
Like a convicted person
In the jail under the jailor.

You have caged me
From my early childhood;
Depriving the amenities of life
Which make the life bright and beautiful.

You have caged me
Like a criminal in the jail.
Who cannot enjoy the life
But to lead a life of hell.

What mischief did I do
For which you put me into the jail?
And command me to obey your order
Without any fail.

You are treating me like a slave,
And beat me now and then.
If I fail to obey you a bit late,
Just like the Jailor in the Jail.

Do you think a little,
What would be happened;
If your position is changed? -
When I shall be free from bondage

And you will be kept in the cage.

ODE ON A SONG

Who is so vile in this world,
That does not love the song.
Which refreshes the mind
From the agony of life?

It has a soothing power of its own,
To bind the friends and foes together;
With the powerful ties of love and sympathy,
Forgetting the enmity of each other.

It is like the current of the river
Which helps the life to flow on its course,
Removing the absurdities of life
Towards the coveted goal.

When the life cannot proceed any further.
And remains stagnant on the way.
The song consoles our mind and inspires us with sweet touch
To proceed the life again removing sorrows and suffering.

The song is a powerful tonic
Which keeps us feet to lead a normal life.
Just like the blood circulation.
Which makes the body alive.

The song knows no death;
And is fresh always.
It gives us a new lease of life
Forgetting the sorrows and sufferings.

ODE ON THE MOSQUITO

I am a mosquito,
I sing my melodious song.
But nobody listens to me
And gives me any thank,

Everyone is praised for sweet song
And earns a lot of remuneration.
But what I received in exchange
Is nothing but utter humiliation.

I am weak in form and feature,
So they care a little for me.
As they are stronger by birth
And I am of low origin.

They condemn me as I suck their blood
But can they think a little for me?
I take my food as little as I can
To maintain my mere existence.

But they are taking beyond their requirement
Depriving their fellow brethren;
Who are going to die without food and drink?
Whereas they are lavishly enjoying.

Who are to be condemned
In the court of judgment.
 Those who are sucking blood like vampire bats
Or who is taking food for mere existence.

ODE ON A ROSE

I am Miss. Rose,
People called me the queen of the flowers.
But it is a pity on me
That I have no beloved lover.

People come to me
To enjoy my beauty
And I give them my sweet company.
Just like a beloved lady.
I cheer them up
Just like a better half.
And redress their grief
With the sparkle of my smile.

I leave no stone unturned
For their entire satisfaction.
But what I received in exchange
Is nothing but disgrace from them.

As I passed my bereaved nights,
In the midst of beautiful surroundings;
Without my beloved lover
In the desolated bower.

Someone molested me
And thrown me out of the bower.
After their sexual enjoyment
Just like a sexual lover.

What a tragic life I lead
Can anyone think of it?

People called me queen
But alas! I have no king.

ODE ON A PET

I have a Pet, Robin Hood by name;
Who accompanied me everywhere.
Just like a faithful follower
With deep love and devotion.

When I was grasped by misfortune
Everyone bade goodbye from me.
Just like the cuckoo in the spring
Who never stayed in the winter to sing.

I became too poor to earn my livelihood.
And passed the days with starvation
Yet he did not leave me alone
And stayed with me like a faithful one.

Once I fell ill and was moaning for death.
He conceived my condition and went to a friend.
But returned with a handful of tears to shed,
By the side of my moaning bed.

Being disappointed, he went to a shop
And stole a piece of loaf.
But he was caught red handed.
And severely beaten on the head;
Which sent him to the house of death
Leaving me alone on the moaning bed.

The news came to me as a bolt from the blue;
Which pierced my heart into pieces
And I breathed my last by heart attack,
With a last prayer to be burnt in the same graveyard

As a mark of sincere love and devotion for each other.

ODE ON THE CLARION CALL

I heard the Clarion call,
Advises me to get myself ready;
For the last journey to the beloved Father
Where lies my permanent shelter.

I have been living here
Just like a caged bird.
Who has no liberty
But to surrender to the cruelty.

My heart knows no bound
As I am returning to my house.
Where my Father is awaiting for me
To receive me cordially.

But tears rolled down from cheek,
When I was reminded of my promise.
As I am to be held accountable
For the entire account of my life.

I would highly praised
If the account found correct.
But I would be severely punished
If the account be otherwise.

I am afraid of the judgment
Passed in the super Supreme Court.
Whether to be rewarded to live in the heaven
Or to be banished from the own abode.

ODE ON A GREEN COCONUT

I am Miss Green coconut
My duty is to quench your thirst.
When you become very tired
And come to me to be relieved at heart.

Being fatigued with the heat
You come under a shed for rest.
I give you my sweet company to make you fresh
Just like a beloved wife to her husband.

My elder sister serves you better
Giving you food and shelter.
And you return to your normal life
Mitigating your lust for hunger.

You fall in love with her
Forgetting my sweet company.
And you prefer her better than me
Enchanted by her beauty.

It is I, who quenched your thirst
And gave you a new lease of life.
But you forget me so easily
What an unthinkable plight.

ODE TO THE ALMIGHTY FATHER

I bow to you my Almighty father;
As you have depicted the Nature in such a manner
That it attracts my attention to her
Just like a devoted lover.

Her eternal youth charms me much.
And I fall in love with her,
Just like a passionate bee,
Falls in love with a blooming flower.

My imagination soars very high,
When I see a multi-coloured butterfly
What a magnificent colouring you made,
I cannot express it in language
Just like a child who can only see and enjoy the beauty
But cannot express it to anybody.

I think, you are the devotee of the beauty;
And your creation is so beautiful-
That it draws our attention to her,
Like a worshipper of Nature.

But the selfish men polluting the Nature for their self interest
And turned the fresh Nature into a polluted one.
Just like the harlots who are polluting themselves.
And pollute the environment with their sinful business.

ODE ON A HIGHLAND LASS

I saw a beautiful highland lass
Singing and dancing in the solitary bower.
She was so beautiful inform and feature
That I cannot distinguish her from a flower.

Her voice was so sweet
That she may be called the queen of the music.
And she danced in such an exquisite manner
That she may be called a heavenly dancer.

The flowers were dancing on their mother's lap
With the dancing of the gentle wind.
She was dancing with the flowers
Thinking herself one of their friends.

I gazed at the sight in such a manner
That I forgot my own existence.
My heart replete with joy
And began to sing and dance.

What a sight I enjoyed in the bower!
No language can express it well.
As it is a matter to be conceived at heart
And not to be expressed in language.

ODE ON A WHITE LADY

Once I saw a beautiful lady
On my way to the rose garden
She was white in colour
Inconformity with her white attire.

She was singing a melodious song
Which overflowed the bower.
I could not check my jocund mood
And began to dance with her.

My heart dances with joy
With her unique dancing.
And I forgot the miseries of life
When I heard her melodious music.

She sang a sweet song
Which impressed me much.
And I remained spellbound
To her melodious sound.

What a beauty I see in the bower!
I can't express it in language.
As it is a matter of perception
And can't be expressed to anyone.

I returned home solitary.
But the music followed me.
And gives me enjoyment,
When I lie on my bereaved bed.

ODE ON ENJOYMENT

If you have a pice,
You should purchase rice.
But if you have two
You should purchase flowers for you.

The rice will supply energy
And helps you to run a race.
But the flower will flourish your mind
And helps you to lead a life of enjoyment.

As a tree cannot be developed without nourishment
So a life cannot be flourished without enjoyment.
It is the nucleus of our life,
Which makes the life alive;
And helps it towards the smooth sailing.

Our life is just like a running train
The train cannot run smoothly towards the destination
If it has no proper fuel.
The life cannot run towards the goal
If it has no enjoyment.

A man cannot live by bread alone.
He requires something more
For the smooth sailing of life;
 Without which the life loses its charm and glamour
And appears before us like the boredom.

ODE ON THE BOSS

I am a lifelong prisoner
In the prison hose of the Earth;
Where I have been banished
From the date of my birth.

My co-mates oppressed me now and then
Without assigning any cause.
When I asked them the reason,
They told me "We are the Boss".

When the oppression crossed the bar of limitation;
I could nothing but shed tears for pain.
They paid no heed to me.
And lashed me again and again.

Being blood stained, I appealed to them
To stop the oppression, but all were in vain.
When the oppression knew no bounds
And followed me like a hound.
I filed a case to the Chief Justice of Heaven
But He ceased to give any verdict
When He heard their names.
As they threatened to kill Him with His fame.

Can anyone tell
To whom shall I appeal again?
And who will judge over my case
To redress my pain?

ODE ON A GALLANT PHILOSOPHER

You are the nucleus of Indian film stars.
And modernize the same achieving much fame.
Just like Kamal Ataturk,
The father of the modern Turk.

You know life is not an empty vessel,
But full of enjoyment.
And you drink the life to the lees.
Leaving aside the dark end.
As the swan takes only the milk
Out of the mixture of milk and water
You have enjoyed the life forgetting sorrows and sufferings
Just like a gallant philosopher.

ODE ON THE UNIVERSAL RELATION

My life will come to an end,
And I may not come here again.
Where shall I go, I do not know;
Whether the Heaven or the Hell.

I have to do a lot of things
For the sake of human beings.
As I have received a human birth
By the benediction of the almighty God.

We have come alone in this world.
And we will depart in the same manner.
Why should we bind ourselves with relations.
Which has no practical implications?

We should have only one relation
And that is a universal one.
All of us are brothers and sisters
And God is our universal Father.

ODE ON THE YOUTH

Youth is the prime time of our life.
It is just like the flow-tide.
The flow-tide overflows the bank,
And fertilizes the land; -
For the good harvest at the end.

The youth fertilizes the life.
And makes it enjoyable to us.
If we make it a proper use
We may harvest good crops.

The overflows of water may cause flood.
And give birth a lot of difficulties.
But if it is controlled from the beginning,
It may yield a lot of opportunities.

It is the seed-time of our life
If we sow good seeds and preserve them,
We may expect a good harvest at the end.
But if we fail, the life will lose its fragrance;
And will no longer be charming to us
Just like a garden without flowers.

ODE ON THE DOWNTRODDEN

I am a little insect.
None pay me any heed.
As I am very little in size.
And they are bigger than me.

They oppressed me now and then
Without assigning any cause.
And threaten me to kill
As they are the mighty Boss.

They think, we are born to be oppressed.
As we belong to the weaker links,
And they are born to dominate over us
As they are as powerful as kings.

But if we assemble together
And from an infantry of our own.
We may dethrone the king of Heaven
And win the victory for the downtrodden.

ODE ON THE DIVINE LOVE OF A MOTHER

The mother elephant met an accident,
When she was crossing the Railway line
With the young one as her companion
For grazing the nearest field.

The young one was severely beaten
By the engine of the running train.
And fall on the ground unconscious
With the moaning sound, "Save me, Mummy".

The mother was shocked at the sight,
And trumpeted again and again;
To assemble the kith and kin together,
As she was quite at a loss.
And cannot decide what to do
To get back the life of her child.

The elephants of the nearby forest
Flocked together from all directions,
When they heard the howling sound.
They took the young elephant to their region
And nursed it day and night
To get back the young ones life.

But when all their efforts were in vain,
They consoled the grieved mother
By pulling the trunk over her head,
As she was severely grief-stricken
With her young one's sudden death.

The mother was so grieved at heart
That she could not utter any word

And fell on the ground with a severe heart attack
Uttering the last word, with the moaning voice,
My dear child, "Is there any utility of my life"?

The kin burst into tears and lined together
To show their last respects to them.
By producing a peculiar vocal sound
Just like that of a Grey hound.

They led a funeral procession with them
And buried the mother and the son;-
In the same graveyard near a church
To commemorate the divine love of a mother
Towards her beloved young one.

ODE ON THE SOBBING HEART

Perhaps this might be my last journey
To this malicious world.
Where people live with hatred for each other
Ignoring the sweet touch of love.

People come here like a swarm of bees
Thinking the world a beehive.
And collect honey day and night
As it is their sole aim in life.

One fine morning, they shocked to see –
That life is not a bed of roses but of thorns;
And none is permanent here
As it is the temporary abode of all.

When they face the stern realities of life
They find nothing but to repent.
As they reached at the fag-end of life
And is too late to do the otherwise.

With the sobbing heart, they depart from the world
Just like the wretched ants;
Who fly in the blazing fire
To meet their ardent desire.

ODE ON THE DARK DEMON

The Sun ascends the throne,
On the eastern horizon;
Defeating the dark demon
At the advent of the dawn.

He fought a fierce fight
With the Demon at night;
For conquering the lost kingdom
From the hands of the deadly demon.

The fight going on and on
With the Sun and the Demon.
The cannon balls fall on the ground
Producing a dreadful sound.

The people of the Earth remains unconscious
And lie on the bed with a dreaded heart.
Just like that of a lifeless corpse.
Who has no sense at all.

They opened their eyes at the dawn
With the rays of the rising Sun,
And could not believe their eyes
As they thought otherwise.

They became very glad
When they found no demon.
To threaten them their lives
Just like a wild beast.

They sang and danced in the mirthful surroundings,
In praise of their Great Grand Father;

Who brought them in the world of light
Defeating the dark demon in a fierce fight.

ODE ON SLEEP

Sleep is the harbinger of peace and tranquillity
To our anguished Heart.
We work by day and sleep at night.
To maintain the equilibrium of mind.

If we work for a longer period
Without any proper sleep.
Our mental health breaks down
And we find no peace of mind.

Sleep is the great refresher.
As she refreshes us from anxieties,
With her sweet touch at night.
Just like that of the beloved wife.

When we are overpowered with anxieties
All our capabilities are kept in the jail.
She comes forward with her magic power
And sets us fit to work again.

Sleep is not waste of time.
It supplies us fresh energy
To cope with the difficulties
That prevent us from achieving the goal of life.

ODE ON THE DIVERSITY

Man lives on the land.
Fish lives in the water.
Birds fly in the sky
But where does the Amphibian?

The crow is cawing.
The cow is lowing.
The ass is braying hard.
But what that of an ant?

The rose smells sweet.
And gives us pleasure in grief.
She conquers our heart
With sweet smell and dance.
Just like a young lover.
But what does the pale flower?

The cuckoo satisfies us
With the melodious song.
And relieved us from sorrows
From the days of yore.
But what do the mosquitoes?

There are seven colours.
Some are white.
Some are red.
But is there any colour
Which is commonly accepted?

Why does the world differ
From one man to another?
And who is maintaining the differences

From the very beginning of the creation?

ODE ON AN AUTOCRAT

Darkness descends first
On this beautiful universe
Light comes later on
As an alternative companion.

When there was no light,
Darkness was the only guide.
And prevails over the universe
Guiding the people at large.

When the people were at a loss,
And could not unveil the truth behind.
They concentrated their mind deeply
And found out the truth of light.

Electricity is a modern invention of science
Which replaces the darkness by light.
And the dark night becomes bright like sunshine.
What a great surprise!

But when the electricity is off,
The darkness becomes deeper.
And prevails over the Earth
Just like an Autocrat.

ODE ON THE SNUFF

I am Miss. pulverizing snuff.
My duty is to keep you free from anxieties.
And to maintain your mental health
Leading a life of enjoyment.

I fall in love with you
When come in close contact;
Forgetting the differences between us
We love each other like a devoted lover.

You come to me with mental agony.
I tried my best to redress your pain
Through my constant kiss
Just like a beloved Miss.

When you become very tired
And cannot do anything properly.
I nurse you with all my might and main.
To regain your lost energy.

With my sincere nursing and devotion
You regained your lost vigour and energy.
And began to work whole heartedly
Like a wounded soldier after recovery.

I make you fit again
But you forget me for my low origin
And cut off all sorts of relations with me
Just like an ungrateful bee.

I may come of a low origin,
But my love is divine.

Can you deny the fact ever?
Please tell me, "My dear lover".

ODE ON A TEA-CUP

I am Miss. Tea cup –
I have a lot of lovers of my own.
They love me so much
That they cannot do anything without my touch.

They come to me like a swarm of bees
With the thirsty heart to drink.
I quenched their thirst with my sweet touch
Just like a devoted lover.

They kissed me repeatedly
When come in close contact
I give the same in exchange
As a token of warm love.

They received a new lease of life
Form a few sips of me
And resumed their daily work
With equal vigour and energy.

I act as a stimulant.
And refresh them from weariness.
Just like the stimulating tonic.
To the weak and ailing patient.

ODE ON THE ANTS

We are the little ants
People give us no importance.
As we are too little in size
And cannot do anything with our might.

They trampled us down under foot
And killed us indiscriminately.
When we ask them the cause of killing
They could nothing but smiling.

They forgot the great maxim, "Unity is strength".
If we are united together under the same banner
And revolt against them.
They will find no place to escape.

Moreover, we are not so weak in mind
Though we are very little in size.
We can easily defeat an infantry
With our consolidated power of enmity.

The age of the Boss is coming to a close
And the downtrodden will ascend the throne.
Replacing the mighty Boss,
Who reigned the world so long.

ODE ON THE LEISURE

We cannot work for a longer period.
If we work without leisure,
Our mind will be monotonous;
And find no pleasure to work.

Our energy will be exhausted,
And activities remain suspended;
Due to continuous work without leisure.
Just like a plane cannot fly in the sky without fuel.

The Plane soars very high in the sky
But it has a limitation of its own.
And it cannot fly in the sky anymore
So drops down on the ground for rest.

The plane takes rest in the aerodrome,
For the preparation of the new journey.
And begins to fly in the sky
With fresh vigour and energy.
We, the human beings, do the same thing;
Just like that of the plane.

When we become very tired,
And cannot work anymore.
We have to take rest to rejuvenate ourselves,
For the next journey with vigour and energy.

Leisure gives us new strength,
Just like the fuel to the plane.
And helps us to reach at the goal of life.
Through continuous struggle to survive.

ODE ON HARMONY

What we need today? - is peace and harmony.
Without which life is valueless, so to say.
And cannot be viable any more
In the midst of sorrows and sufferings.

If the world goes on malice for longer,
It will lose its beauty and fragrance.
And turned into the battle field of war monger;
Where there is no place for fellow feeling –
Which is the pre-condition of harmonious living.

We have come to this world,
To fulfil His mission of "one world-one nation".
Thinking the world a single mansion
Where we are to live with deep love and devotion.
But what we see in practice? –
There is no peace and harmony in life.
And we cannot think for each other
Though we belong to the same family.

The world has turned into a den of beasts.
And fighting for each other for supremacy;
Forgetting the basic principle of peace and harmony.
Which binds the people together
And helps to lead a harmonious life.

ODE ON THE GREATEST ARTIST

God is the greatest artist of the world.
And depicts the creation after His fashion
Which attracts our attention in such a manner
That we remained spellbound.

His artistic pleasure is unparalleled;
And none can be compared with Him.
As He is the source of all paintings –
From the meanest to the largest things.

When we look at His magnificent creation
With the inner eyes to see its beauty.
Our hearts replete with pleasure
And began to dance with romantic motion.

He has created this objective world
With a definite aim in view.
Which gives us pleasure and enjoyment
And to see everything – a new.

He loves His creation so much
That He cannot bear its separation.
And He always lives with His creation
Thinking it an inseparable one.

His creation gives us a new vision
Through which we observe everything.
It unfolds a new meaning of cosmogony
Which was hitherto unveiled.

It pleases us at every step.
Either in love or in disappointment.

And guides us as the Pole-star
In the midst of sorrows and enjoyment.

ODE ON A TRAIN

The train runs with the passengers
From one station to the other.
And helps them to alight at the destination
With perfect ease and satisfaction.

The train knows no rest and goes apace.
Just like a running horse
Until to reach at the destination
With full speed and vigour.

She takes all possible cares
For the safety of the passengers.
Even at the cost of her life
She saves the passengers with all her might.

When we go to a distant land,
She runs as far as she can;
To reach at the destination in time
Toiling all day and might.

If she reaches a bit late,
She will be held responsible;
For hampering the others interest
Though she is in ill health.

She cares a little for her health
And is running to time.
To avert the criticism of passengers
And that of her sister running behind.

She teaches us the dictums of punctuality,
And inspires us to follow them verbatim;

If we wish to lead a prosperous life
Through the proper use of time.

If we use our time properly,
Our life will be flourished.
But if we do the otherwise,
The life will be blemished.

ODE ON A LAMENTED BUTTERFLY

Once I saw a multicolored butterfly
Flying over my head-
Conveying the death of her beloved
Through an inaudible voice.

She was sobbing herself to grief
To lighten her heart to the public.
But nobody came to console her
As she is alone in this world.

Her beloved is no more with her.
And went to the heavenly abode
Leaving her in deep distress
In this mournful world alone.

Her grief mounts so high
That she cannot check herself
And was moved to tears
For her beloved's bereavement.

The butterfly is a bird of beauty
And is a unique creation of the Almighty.
But all her beauty fades away
With the death of her beloved.

She has turned into an ugly bird
Losing her beauty and color.
Just like the widows of our society
Who have been deprived of all.

When she was with her beloved
She had all embellishments.
And everybody would come to her
To enjoy her beauty and charms.
But after the death of her beloved
She assumed a gloomy attitude.
And nobody comes to see her
As she is very ugly to look.

ODE ON THE AUTOBIOGRAPHY OF AN UMBRELLA

I protect you from sunshine and rain
When you are walking on the street.
And try to present you an enjoyable life
Through my sincere service.

When the April sun rises above your head
And exercises excessive heat.
I take the heat upon my body
To release you from the fatigue.

When the showers came in torrents
And try to drench you through and through
I prevent you from the torrential rain
Getting myself thoroughly drenched.

I leave no stone unturned
To give you a comfortable life.
Like a devoted servant
I serve you all the while.

But alas! You forget my sincere service
Which I rendered you for so many years.
And left me alone in the dustbin
To pass away the rest of my life with tears.

ODE ON THE WILD ANIMALS

People called us wild animals,
As we are living in the forest.
And lead an uncivilized life
Which the people cannot expect.

They called us ferocious animals,
As we are guided by the ferocity
And leave a little space for civility
As we are not at all civilized.

We do everything at our passion's call.
And cannot resist ourselves from doing any wrong.
As we are not rectified like human beings
Who are conscious enough to do or undo anything.

They pride themselves on the privileged birth
As they are the best creation of God.
And reigning over the world monopoly
Ignoring the others' demand.

But it is a matter of regret to us all –
To see the behavior of the monopolists,
Who have turned the beautiful world
Into the ugly den of the beasts.

They are working for their own interest
Leaving out the interest of others.
And trying to maintain their supremacy
By inventing the dreadful arms.

We are surprised to see their rationality,

Which leads them towards the path of destruction.
In place of building a prosperous Nation
They are being guided by self-reservation.

ODE ON THE UNPRIVILEGED

We, the smallest innocent beings
Living in the world of the Privileged.
Where we have no right to live in.
As we belong to the unprivileged.

The Privileged think themselves superior to all
And they can do or undo anything
At their beck and call
As they are all in all.

They are maintaining their existence
At the cost of others.
But they neglect them everywhere
As they are the big brothers.

The unprivileged are toiling hard
To maintain their livelihood.
But it is a matter of regret
They are going on without food.

They are producing food
But have no right to consume.
Just like the worker bees
Who are working for the queens.

ODE ON A NEGLECTED CANDLESTICK

I am a neglected candlestick,
I try my best to remove darkness,
In a fierce fight with the daemon
When there is no light in the prison.

Though my light is dim
In comparison with the others.
Yet I leave no stone unturned
To give you pleasure.

I love you with deep devotion
Just like a rustic girl,
Who loves her lover
From the core of her heart.

You neglect me now and then
As I come of a low origin.
But think a little while
My love is really divine.

I serve you at a time
When there is none by your side.
Just like a faithful friend
Who serves you in need.

My love is selfless.
As I demand nothing in exchange
Just like a sweet flower
Who demands nothing for her smell.

ODE ON THE SINKING SHIP

I am a nameless ship
Without any rudder
I move hither and thither
But find no harbor.

I am toiling day and night
To find out the harbor.
But I find it nowhere
What a painful pleasure!

I am trying my best without any rest,
To revive my connection with the Father;
Who controls my activities
Just like a doll by the juggler.

As ill luck would have it,
I failed my connection with Him.
And floating over the sea
Just like a helpless baby.

I cried again and again for help
As I am going to sink in the sea.
Just like a helpless baby
Who does not know how to swim.

Tears rolled down from my cheek,
As I find no other magic.
To draw the attention of the Father
Who is my only savior.

ODE ON THE CHURCH BELL

The Bell rings in the church
Announcing the time of prayer.
As we are engaged elsewhere
Forgetting the beloved Father.

The Father sends us here,
To preach His noble ideas;
Among the wretched people
Who are out of gear.

Life is not full of empty dreams
Of fruitless efforts.
But the tale of sacrifice
For the benefit of mankind.

He wants a prosperous world
With the cooperation of each other.
Just like the members of a joint family.
Who labored hard for its prosperity.

If we do the otherwise
The Father will be furious;
And will sentence us to imprisonment,
As a punishment of our disobedience.

ODE ON THE CHRISTMAS DAY

The Christmas day is a day for enjoyment,-
Not only for the Christian community
But it is a day for love and harmony
For the entire humanity.

As on this day, God sent His beloved Son
From the Heaven to this Earth;
To save the people of the world at large
Who are in confrontation with each other.

He came to bind the people of the World
With the ties of the universal brotherhood.
And to rescue the world from the hands of the war monger.
Who turned it into the slaughter house.

He sacrificed his life to the alter of Peace,
Which inspired us to give up malice.
And to lead the life of peaceful co-operation
Avoiding the life of hatred and confrontation.

It is a day of promise for sacrifice,
For the betterment of downtrodden;
Who are very near and dear to us
As we belong to the same Father.

ODE ON THE BEAUTY OF DARKNESS

What is Beauty – can anyone tell?
As it depends upon the mentality of men.
How can we distinguish between beauty and ugliness?
As there is no such measurement.

Someone see beauty in one thing
But the others consider it ugly.
As it has no universal acceptance
Though all of us run after beauty.

A beauteous thing is a joy forever.
And it flashes upon our inward eye.
The eye decides the beauty of a thing
Through its devotional findings.

Someone see beauty in the rising sun
And someone see it on its setting.
The eye camera shows us the beauty of a thing
As it is really very confusing.

Everything has beauty of its own
And nothing of this world is ugly.
We are to see it to the proper perspective
As the world is full of beauty.

The beauty of darkness is really exciting
In comparison to that of others.
As it appeals to our inner mind
And gives us a thrilling impression.

The beauty of darkness leads us to the Heaven

And it connects both Heaven and Earth together.
And we find no place for ugliness.
As Beauty prevails everywhere.

ODE ON DREAMS

Our life is full of dreams -
 Some are black in color,
And some are evergreen.
It makes the life viable
And gives us enjoyment
Through sorrows and sufferings.

It is like the current of the river
Which overflows the mind.
And gives us pleasure
Just like a blooming flower.

Dream is our faithful friend
And guides us towards the goal.
Defeating the hindrances on the path of prosperity
Which beset the life as a whole.

Life is not a bed of roses but of thorns.
We are to overcome those with repeated endeavors.
If we fail to overcome those problems,
The life will not find its coveted goal.
And we cannot enjoy the life with all its flavors
In spite of all our repeated endeavors.

ODE ON PATRIOTISM

A true patriot is he
Who loves his motherland,
Just like his own mother
With deep love and devotion.

He should sacrifice his own passions
At the altar of his motherland.
And leaves no stone unturned
For her all round development.

He should save her from foreign attack
And to uphold her prestige and dignity.
Even at the cost of his life
He should work for her integrity.

The mother serves him for a certain period
But the motherland serves him
From the cradle to the grave.
And makes his life enjoyable
Affording all sorts of enjoyment.

When he is fatigued with the Sun,
She gives him shed to overcome;
And when he is hungry for food,
She offers him a lot of fruits.
To quench his thrust, she serves him water.
Just like the beloved mother.

When he is in deep distress
None comes to redress his pain.
But she affords him a comfortable environment

To maintain his mental health.
With flowery bower and greenness.
She helps him to lead a comfortable life
In the midst of natural surroundings.

None can repay her debt,
As she is our beloved mother.
And helps us every now and then
For our all-round development.

ODE ON DEATH

Death is our bosom friend.
As she vanishes the sufferings for good;
Which makes our life painful
From the very beginning of childhood.

It nourishes our body and mind,
And gives us invaluable suggestions,
For doing everything in time.
Within the sphere of life.

If we neglect in doing everything in time
It will never be completed.
And our life will come to an end
When we have nothing but to be repented.

Death is the rudder of our life,
Which regulates our activities;
From the cradle to the grave.
To make the life viable.

The Death leads us towards the Heaven
Where resides the beloved Father.
And He will take account of our duties
Which were entrusted upon.

ODE ON A FRIEND IN NEED

My dear constant companion, I welcome you;
For giving your constant help in molding my life,
Relieving me from the mental agony
Just like a devoted wife.

My friends and relatives come to me
When I am in better days.
And bid good-bye from me
When I fall in deep distress.

They are like the cuckoo in the spring
And never stayed with me in the chilly winter.
But you are always in close touch with me
And tried your best to remove the distress.

When I fall in the hands of Misfortune
You come forward for my help.
And comfort me now and then.
Just like a faithful friend.

I cannot repay your invaluable help,
Which you are rendering me constantly;
For the development of my mental health.
And to save me from the jaws of Death.

When my mental agony rise so high
As I cannot sleep on the bed.
You come forward with your helping hand;
And help me to sleep peacefully.

Your heart is full of wisdom.

And I tried my best to acquire it,
Through your constant kiss and boundless love
Bestowed upon me day and night.

"A friend in need is a friend in deed" –
There goes the mighty proverb.
You have proved it through your active help and self-sacrifice
During the whole course of my life.

ODE ON THE ECHOING GREEN

I love the echoing green,
Where I played with the mates;
Forgetting the racial differences
We embraced each other like friends.

We played in the echoing green
With equal vigor and harmony.
Just like the members of the joint family
Which knows no disunity.

The old folk witnessed our game
And burst into laughter.
When we embraced each other
After the game was over.

They recollected their past days
When they were players like us.
And played in the echoing green
With equal vigor and enthusiasm.

Those days are gone
As they have crossed the bar.
And would not be able to have them again
In spite of their earnest endeavor.

Had they regain their youth again!
They would have consumed it to the fullest extent;
To make their life bright and beautiful;
With the vigor and energy of the youth.

ODE ON THE TEMPTATION

The very name of my beloved
Strikes my imagination.
And soars so high in the sky
That it forgets the habitation.

It soars up in such a lofty place
Where there is no selfish men,
And people live here with fellow feeling
Like fellow brethren.

We are living in the den of beasts
Unfit for human habitation.
And people fall here at every step
In the hands of mighty temptation.

Temptation is the very breath of our life.
It has an overwhelming power.
And none can resist it
Like Adam and Eve.

Temptation makes our life miserable.
But yet we persisted in.
Just like a camel eating prickly shrub,
In spite of profuse bleeding.

ODE ON THE NURSING MOTHER

I love you my Nursing Mother
From the core of my heart.
As you are nursing me day and night
From the date of my birth.

You are supplying me pure sweet drink,
Just like a mother to her child.
And I drink it to my heart's content.
To enrich my body and mind.

You are rendering me the amenities of life
To make my life enjoyable.
And I am leading a life of peace and progress
With your active participation and help.

I played on your lap like a little chap
From the cradle to the grave.
And you have inspired me to win the battle of life
In a fierce fight with the opponents.

I never forget your kindness
Which showed me the path to progress.
And I achieved the goal of life
Through your sincere help.

Your heart is full of honey
Like that of a Bengali mother.
And I drink it to my heart's content.
Just like a glutton in the dinner.

Tears rolled down from my cheeks

When you flashed in my memory.
I could not console the anguished heart
That cries for you bitterly.

ODE ON THE SWEET LADY

My dear Sweet Lady,
How sweet you are!
My heart dances with ecstasy
When I see you in the bower.

You are full to the brim of your youth
Which enchanted me thoroughly.
And I become mad with your beauty
Just like a hungry bee.

I like to play with you
In the solitary bower.
Just like Romeo and Juliet.
Who were ideal lover.

When my grieved heart
Finds no pleasure
I look and look at you
To relieve my anguished heart.

Tears rolled down from my cheeks
Like summer tempest
As I find no consolation
To get rid of the bereavement.

Alas! If I were in sleep!
And never come back to dreary life
I would have enjoyed your sweet company
Throughout the eternity.

ODE ON THE LITTLE

Little drops of rain
Make the vast ocean.
Little grains of sand
Make the pleasant land.

Little acts of kindness
May save the life of a man.
And our heart dances with joy
When we remind the kind acts.

A little cooperation of the individuals
Give us an integrated society.
And helps us to lead a prosperous life
Free from the jaws of poverty.

A little fragment of beautiful marbles
Make the finest Taj Mahal.
Which draws our attention so much
That we called it one of the wonders of the world.

Little paints of color
Make a beautiful picture
Which appeals to our heart
As a joy forever.

A little daisy flower
Gives us immense pleasure
And makes our life enjoyable
In the debris of dark despair.

A little touch of sympathy

May remove the sorrows and sufferings, -
And helps us to live together
Forgetting the racial boundaries.

A little fellow feeling amongst us
May lead us towards the harmonious life.
And gives us fresh energy and vigor
To build a malice-free society.

Nothing little of this world
Can never be neglected.
We can build our mighty nation
On the consolidate foot step.

Unity is strength
And disunity brings disasters.
We can learn this lesson
From the life of the little ants.

ODE ON THE SOUL

Soul is the integral part of a Body.
Without soul the body is useless.
And looks like an empty vessel
In spite of all its embellishments.

It is just like the Sun without the rays.
The Sun without rays is nothing but a fun.
And is incapable of giving any light
For the benefit of mankind.

The ray is the source of energy and vigor
And gives the Sun its motivation.
Without rays the sun becomes lifeless.
And loses all its charms.

Soul is our guiding spirit.
And guides us towards the fulfillment of life.
Without soul the life cries in the wilderness,
And finds no way towards its fulfillment.

Soul is the source of our inspiration
And inspires us to achieve the lofty ideas,
Without which the life has no charm
And becomes drudgery and dull.

The soul is immortal and knows no death
It can only be transferred from the old to the new one.
Leaving its existence all the same
When the world comes to an end.

A soulless life is a song less lyre.

It can, in no way "produce any song"
For giving enjoyment to the anguished heart.
Though the lyre remains intact.

ODE ON HIS KINDNESS

God is all merciful
And loves all alike.
Just like the beloved father
Loves his dear child.

He is our eternal father
And keeps us all alive.
With deep love and devotion
Which is hard to find.

We are very near and dear to Him
As His love is all pervading.
And binds us together
With the ties of fellow feeling.

He gives us inspiration,
To follow the path of truth.
Removing the absurdities of life
Which lead us towards the life of a brute.

He forgives us from the core of His heart,
For committing crimes time and again;
If we confess guilt to Him
And beg for His kindness.

He is our benevolent Father
And stretches His hands to help.
In maintaining the solidarity
For our all-round development.

His heart leaps with joy

When we are in prosperity.
And his eyes shed a lot of tears
When we are in calamity.

Our life is a vessel without any rudder,
And cannot move anywhere;
Without His active participation.
Just like a Rudderless ship to the harbor.

He is the pilot of our life,
And piloting us properly;
To reach the destination in time
And to make the life sublime.

We should remain grateful to Him
For His active help and participation.
In molding our life and character
After His own fashion.

ODE ON RELIGION

The religion is the one and the same
Though it assumes different names.
But the content remains the same
Just like water and the rains.

All roads lead to Rome
From different directions of their own.
But the goal remains unchanged
Though the directions may be different.

"Religion" is a unified term
And helps the people to unite together
Under the banner of the Religion.
People lead a life of happy union.

Forgetting the racial identity
The people flocked together for unity.
Under the spiritual guidance of the preceptor
They lead a life of spirituality.

Religion means being and becoming,
Without hampering others' entity.
And to lead a harmonious life
For the betterment of the society.

Religion shows us the path of truth
Removing the brute ness of mind.
And turned the world into the holy abode,
Where there is no place of malice.

A religious life goes apace

Like the rivers to the seas.
And makes our life fruitful
Achieving the eternal bliss.

Religion flows in the veins
Like blood circulation.
And gives us pleasant life
Removing the impurities of Heart.

ODE ON A FOSTER CHILD

I do not know my parentage
And live here alone.
I find no friend to comfort me
And lead a tragic life of my own.

People called me foster child
As my birth is not known.
And insult me now and then
Asking my father's name.

Being insulted by the neighbors
I became very sad.
And made up my mind to commit suicide.
Because of the mysterious dad.

I shed a lot of tears
And prayed to the almighty Father.
To solve the mystery of my birth
Before my fellow neighbors.

I prayed and prayed but no results,
And going to die from starvation.
Still the mystery of my birth remains in the dark
Because of the mysterious dad.

On the seventh day of my starvation,
I fell on the ground unconscious.
And a vision came before me
To unfold the mystery of my birth.

My heart leaps with joy

And dissolved into ecstasy;
When I found my beloved father
Who was so longer in the mystery.

ODE ON THE NATURE

Nature is our faithful friend, philosopher and guide.
As she guides us towards the goal of life.
From the very birth to the grave She renders us help;-
And her constant help presents us a blissful life
For which we are really grateful to her.
As She guides us at every work of life;-
And helps us towards its perfection.
Without which we cannot reach at the destination.

Nature is the part and parcel of our life.
As we cannot do anything without her help.
All our hopes and aspirations will be nipped in the bud
If the nature does not help us.

So both of us are intermingled with each other,
And we cannot expect our separation at any cost.
Without Nature's active cooperation -
We cannot expect our existence in the world.
So nature is our unfailing friend, philosopher and guide
And we should be grateful to her throughout the life.

Nature is our nursing mother,-
And nurses us day and night –
To make our life enjoyable to us
Supplying all sorts of amenities of life.

When we become hungry she provides us food.
And when we are fatigued with the heat of the Sun
She provides us shelter under the shade of the trees.
Which refreshes our body and mind at the same time.

Nature is the pleasure garden.
And presents us pleasant life, -
Removing the sorrows and sufferings
Which vitiate our fresh mind.

A fresh mind is just like the fresh wind,-
Which gives us immense pleasure.
To lead a prosperous life of our own;
Finding out the "hidden treasure" –
Where lies the ultimate goal.

It gives us fresh energy
To motivate our life ahead.
Leaving aside the absurdities
Just like the fuel to the train.

Nature never betrays the heart
That loves her with deep love and devotion.
She keeps the heart fresh for ever
Just like the blood circulation.

As the nature helps us for our all-round development;-
So we should do everything for her embellishment.
If we fail to do our duty for the survival of the nature –
We can't expect our existence in the world.

We should take all sorts of possible cares
To save the nature from the hands of pollution.
If the nature is polluted, everything will be polluted;
And the human race will come to an end.
Which is not at all desirable for us
As we interdependent with each other.

ODE ON THE RAIN

Little drops of Rain
Fertilize the land.
And help to grow more crops
Even in the barren land.

The Rain gives up cool shade
To protect us from Heat,
Just like the beloved mother
Protects her child.

The showers of rain fall on the ground,
As the showers of kindness.
And the Earth rejuvenated herself
With the advent of the Rain.

The Earth quivers with life
With the sweet touch of the showers.
And turns it into the granary of the Green.
Forgetting the dreary hours.

The flowers begin to blossom
Forgetting the weariness.
And danced like the maidens
In the respective branches.

They attacked our attention
With their natural beauty.
Our heart is affluent with joy
And dances with dignity.

The bees are humming

To have a close touch
And fly over the bower
For gossiping with the lover.

A poet cannot but be gay
In such a mirthful company.
And he merged with the Nature
Forgetting his individuality.

His heart is flooded with mirth
Leading him to the Ecstasy.
And he sings a sweet song
To wash away the despondency.

ODE ON THE FEIGNED LOVER

A feigned lover is a poisonous snake.
And bites us now and then in the guise of a friend.
She makes our life drudgery and dull
Projecting the venom throughout the Heart.

We fall in love with the feigned lover
Enchanted by her outward beauty.
She takes advantage of our innocence
And dragged us down to the dignity.

We are caught in the net of love
Just like the fish in the water.
And find no way to get rid of her
In spite of the repeated endeavors.

Her poisonous biting gives us pain
Which we cannot endure any longer.
And the life appears a burden to us
Losing all its beauty and flavor.

Our life is caught in the trap
Just like a bird in the cage.
And forgets the free movements
Being cut off from the rest.

Our life comes to an end
Through continuous struggle.
But we never find the goal of life
And cry in the wilderness.

ODE ON THE DEEP SEA

Our life is sailing over the sea
Just like the boats on the river.
It sailed as rapidly as it can
When we are very younger.

Our life is at stake
When it sails in the turbulent ocean.
And cannot find out the destination.
Though it sailed with more devotion.

Our life is nothing but a sailing boat
Which is sailing day and night.
And we are to maintain our existence
Throughout the fierce fight.

If we win in the battle of life,
Our life will be crowned with success.
But if we meet defeat in the battle
Our life will come to an end.

We are born soldiers
In the battle of life.
And we are to struggle hard
To achieve the goal in time.

If we fail to reach at the goal
Through continuous struggle.
Our life will meet a crushing defeat.
And find no embellishment.

The life will not find its coveted goal
If it failed to sail smoothly.
And will lose its integrity
Sinking into the deep sea.

ODE ON THE SWAN-SONG

Our life is full of vigor
When we are younger.
And knows no rest
Running after the wealth and fame.

But when the youth is gone
It takes a different turn.
And begins to flow on its course
With slow motion from the source.

We, no longer, run after the golden deer.
As it is a fruitless effort.
And gives us no perfection of life
Which we need for the other world.

Our running after Fame; -
Has come to an end.
And we concentrate our mind
To find out the goal of life.

But it is too late to run apace
As our energy is exhausted.
And failed to find out the goal of life
Due to old age and feeble mind.

Our life has come to an end
Running after wealth and fame.
And sings a doleful song.
Lamenting over the fruitless effort.

Our life sings the swan-song

Not to run after the wealth and fame
But to find out the goal of life
From the beginning of the voyage.

ODE ON A STREET BEGGAR

I am a street beggar
Begging from door to door.
But none show me any sympathy,
As I am extremely poor.

I am begging from sunrise to sunset
But my wallet remains empty.
Tears rolled down from my cheeks
When I think of the famished family.

Being tired and hungry
I came to a rich man's house.
None gave me food and shelter
And turned me out.

I began to walk and walk
In prospect of alms.
But my fate betrays me
And I began to run in the Sun.

Being fatigued with the Sun
I could step no further.
And slept on the ground
Being overpowered with hunger.

People trampled me under foot
Just like rotten goods.
And showed me no kindness
As I put on dirty dress.

They kicked me out of their way

As I disturbed them at every step.
And abused me with slang words
Just like a street dog.

I found no place to hide myself
In this wide universe.
None showed me any sympathy
Providing food and shelter.

Poverty has snatched me away
From all sorts of privileges.
And banished me from the society
Due to my chill penury and old age.

I have no place in the animal world.
As I am a foreigner to them.
And find no place in the society
As I am a downtrodden.

My life is at a stake
Finding no place anywhere
Where shall I go now
And who will provide me shelter?

ODE ON THE SINCERE SERVICE

I am badly engaged in my duty
From the sunrise to the sunset.
People hailed from different places
To have my requisite help.

They queued up before me
To have my sincere service.
And I rendered them my usual help
Who are awaiting for the train.

I bid them goodbye
When they get into the train.
They waved their hands in gratitude
With a promise to come here again.

I looked at them in the running train
As long as they were in the view.
And I turned a mournful turn
When I found another queue.

I find no time to sleep
And go on without drink.
As I badly engaged
To serve the people for the train.

I am greatly inspired by the dictum,
"To serve man is to serve God".
And I think my life is a great success, -
When I serve God through the service of men.

ODE ON THE TRAGEDY

Tragedy gives us the true taste of life
Which we cannot find in the comedy alone.
As it gives us only the partial view
Which in no way, be called the life; a true.

When we dive down into the inner life
We may see the hidden treasures.
Just like the divers see the pearls
When they dive down into the ocean.

We are to enjoy the life with all its sufferings,
Otherwise, the life will be meaningless.
And we cannot enjoy it in the true sense,-
As life is an excellent blend of pleasure and pain.

We are to drink life to the lees,
 For our perfect satisfaction.
As it is the gift of the great architect
Which we cannot enjoy after death.

Life is the strange mixture of will and woe.
We are to accept both of them,-
With equal vigor and temperament;
To make the life a great success.

Pain and pleasure is the spice of life
Which gives us thrilling experience.
Without pain the life has no charm of its own
Just like a lady without the charming face.

Tragedy makes our life more meaningful

And gives us a new insight to unfold the truth.
We are to struggle hard through pain and pleasure
To enjoy the life with indomitable valor.

ODE ON THE GOALLESS LIFE

I do not like to live,
I do not like to die;
I only wish to be flourished
In the fertile minds of men.

Man comes only once
In this world so beauty.
And bids goodbye from it,
Just finishing his duty.

All of us are passersby
Coming here to pass away
Leaving the antiquities of our life
Just like the river on her way.

If we pass away from this world
Without leaving any impression of our own.
Our life will be useless as flood water
And will not find its coveted goal.

A goalless life is a rudderless ship,
Which can move on the ocean;
With equal vigor and motion
But cannot reach at the destination.

ODE ON THE DEJECTED LOVER

When I was full to the brim of my youth
I had a lot of lovers of my own.
Who loved me so dearly
That I could not expect my existence alone.

I was moved with their love.
Just like that of the better half.
And unlocked my heart to them,
They behaved, "we are one and the same".

I was so deep in love with them –
That I could not spend a single moment,
Without their happy union in the forest.
Just like Romeo and Juliet.

I spent many a joyful spring
When my youth was full to the brim.
They enjoyed my beauty to the heart's content.
Thinking me a blessed damsel.

But when I lost my youth,
I lost my embellishments.
And they left me alone in the bower
For condoling over my happy hours.

ODE ON THE IMAGINATION

Man is imaginative by nature.
We can't expect any creative activity
Without the sweet touch of imagination.
As it is the mother of all innovations.

Without imagination the life loses its charms.
And appears before us like a boredom –
Where there is no place for romantic flavor.
Without which the life finds no fervor.

We like to see everything with our own eyes
But our vision is limited to a certain extent.
And we can't see beyond that limitation.
Without the help of colorful imagination.

Where the vision fails, the imagination creeps up
To fulfill the unfulfilled ambition.
As imagination leads us towards the perfection
Of our extinguished thoughts and desires.

Imagination gives us new taste of life.
And leads us towards the Romantic world.
Where we find the life in the true sense of the term
With all its varied tastes and colors.

Imagination is the great refresher
Of our anguished heart.
And refreshes us through its sweet touch.
Just like that of a beloved lover.

ODE ON THE DEPARTED FATHER

My father is no more with me
He has gone to his own abode,
Leaving me in the turbulent sea
How shall I live here alone?

He was my friend, philosopher and guide.
And guided me towards the destination.
I followed him like an obedient pupil
To fulfill my hopes and aspirations.

My life is at a stake in deep sea of trouble.
As I don't know how to swim in the sea,
And how to get rid of the problems –
With which I terribly infested.

Tears rolled down like summer tempest,
When I remind his valuable help.
He loved me as an affectionate son
And I loved him as my beloved father.

I am crying bitterly like a helpless child.
But none comes to show me the path of life.
How shall I proceed towards the gloomy future?
As I have no friend and philosopher.

ODE ON THE VISION OF LIFE

Everyone must have a vision of life.
Without vision the life has no charm,
And appears drudgery and dull; -
Just like a tree without any flower.

A visionless life, is a rudderless ship;
Which can only move aimlessly hither and thither,
But cannot reach at the harbor.
And becomes a total failure.

Vision leads a man towards the fulfillment of life
Just like a mother leads her child –
To be a grown up man in the society
With all its capabilities fully flourished.

Our life is a budding flower.
We have to try our best to give it a blooming shape
With deep love and devotion.
Through colorful imagination.

Man is the architect of his own fate.
His life is molded through the vision.
And take a definite shape of perfection
When transforms into thought of action.

ODE ON THE PREPARATION FOR DEATH

Our life is a strange preparation for Death
We are slowly but surely advancing towards it,
As it is the ultimately goal of our life;
And none of us can permanently survived.

From the very moment of our birth,
We hear the footstep of the Death;
And we begin to cry bitterly to avoid it –
But none can escape from its hand.
As it is universally accepted.

If we born, we have to die;
There goes the mighty proverb
And there is no other alternative to it,
As it is promulgated by the Almighty.

When we born in this world,
We are to prepare ourselves for Death;
Just like a student prepares his lesson
In order to cut a good figure in the examination.

If the student fails to prepare his lesson well,
He will cut a very sorry figure in the examination;
And will surely be repented in the long run,
For failure in the examination.

Similarly, if we, the people of the world;-
Forget to prepare our life for death;
Our life will never be crowned with success,
And we are to shed tears at the fag-end.

ODE ON THE DEPARTED SOUL

Oh! My dear departed soul,
Where is your new abode?
I failed to search it out
In the dreary world around.

Where people are no better than beasts,
And lead a very sordid life;
Which is no way, can be called ;-
The sensible life of a man at all.

As they only know how to eat and drink
Leaving aside the bliss of life;
Without which no life can be perfect
And would not be able to reap the harvest.

When you gave me your company
My mind was full to the brim in glee.
And danced like the Daffodils
In the breeze of the spring time.

I enjoyed your heavenly love,
Like a child from its mother;
Which embellished my heart with charity,
And gave me a thrilling touch of ecstasy.

You are no more with me.
My life has turned into a desert,
Where there is no Oasis and cuckoo bird
To ease my doleful heart with a sweet song.

My mind has lost its flavor,

And is no longer enjoyable to me.
As a Honey less pale flower
Can hardly draw the attention of the bee.

My eyes shed constant tears,
Just like a sobbing deer.
None come to show me any sympathy
Where lies the tragedy.

ODE ON THE STRUGGLE OF LIFE

Life is not a bed of roses but of prickly thorns.
From the very birth on the Earth to the grave,
We are to face lot of troubles to overcome
With indomitable courage and robust optimism,
To enjoy the life with all its varied tastes and colors.
Like that of a winning soldier in the war.

Our life is a battle field and all of us are soldiers.
We are to fight tooth and nail to win over.
Otherwise the life will lose its charms and flavors,
And will no longer be enjoyable to us,
Like that of a faded flower.

If we fail to win over the battle of life,
Our life will be doomed forever.
And will find no way to be flourished for the future,
Just like that of the captive in the war.

A captive is no better than a bird in the cage,
As none of them has liberty to move freely;
And to express the heart to the fellow brethren.
But to lead a miserable life in the bondage.

ODE ON THE KINDNESS

Kindness prevails in the mind
Like the flow-tide of the river.
And sweeps away the garbage of life
Like that of the Ganges water.

It purifies the mind like a true Purifier
Banishing the debris of dark despair.
And provides fresh energy and vigor
To lead the life as fresh forever.

It has a magic power to flow from one mind to another
And to replete the heart with fresh enjoyment;-
Removing the sorrows and sufferings inherent.
Just like the loving mother to her children.

It removes the darkness of the mind,
Through enkindling the light of merriment.
And the mind gets back a new lease of life
To lead the life a fresh again.

When Force fails to conquer the Heart
Kindness appears on the stage.
And it plays its role winning the Soul.
Just like a successful actress.

Kindness is our faithful friend.
And helps now and then without self interest
In molding the life as we desired
From the very birth towards the end.

It bears a selfless character of its own.

And serves the people at large,
Without considering friends and foes.
Just like that of a blooming flower
Which distributes its fragrance to one and all.

ODE ON THE UNIVERSAL BROTHERHOOD

My life is limited to a certain extent.
And it cannot be extended any more.
I am to use properly every moment of life,
For the benefit of the mankind as a whole.

My family spreads all over the world.
None of them is alien to me.
All of them are my brothers and sisters
As they belong to same Family.

My religion is a universal one.
And it is to do good for others –
Indiscriminating friends or foes.
As I am directed by the Heavenly Father.
When I came down to this Earth.

My mission is to serve the downtrodden
Who have none to help.
And lead a very miserable life
Which no language can tell.

There will be no space for the rich and the poor.
As they inherited from the same Father.
And the wealth will be equally distributed
Among all the sons and daughters.
As all of them are co-sharers.

If the world proceeds in this way of mutual cooperation.
The fear of war will find no place to exist.
And the people will lead a life of Heavenly bliss
Banishing the selfishness as a social crime.

ODE ON THE EQUILIBRIUM

A fierce fight going on between the Rain and the Sun
For gaining supremacy over the sky to reign.
Fighting going on and on but the result remains unsettled ,-
As both of them are equally strong in body and mind.

None can defect other in the fight
And the fight going on for a pretty while.
Moreover, it is a question of prestige to them
Who will be defeated and who will be at the helm.

The Sun tried its best to dry up the Rain.
And the Rain tried to drench the Sun with its water.
In this way, the duel between the Rain and the Sun going on;
But none can defeat the other in the Horizon.

At last the Air came to compromise the unending fight.
And appear before them with all its might and main.
An honorable treaty was signed between them
In order to declare the unending fight to an end.

The treaty was written by the Sun beam with its different colors.
 In presence of the Air, the mighty harbinger.
And it was accepted by both of them as an amicable settlement
To dominate the sky by turns with the written chart.

From the beginning of the Earth, the Treaty is in vogue,
The Sun and the Rain give it due importance.
And the world goes apace year after year
Maintaining the great law of the Equilibrium.

ODE ON THE MUSIC OF WORDS

Music is the very breath of our life,
Without which we cannot expect our existence.
It makes our life viable on the Earth.
So we are to give it due importance.

Music is inherent in everything,
Even it presents in the meanest being.
Without music the world cannot move apace.
And remains stagnant being lifeless.

Music is the great refresher of our Mind.
And it refreshes us form the agony of life.
When we fall in deep distress,
It soothes our mind like a faithful friend.

Music is life and Life is Music.
Both of them are inseparable from the other.
Just like a river from the Water.
It is an integrated thing and is indivisible in nature.

We can't expect a melodious life without music.
As it is an omnipotent Phenomenon of the Universe
Which inspires us at every step of life
And molded it at its sweet will.

Music can be classified into two types;
One is inaudible and the other is audible.
This audible music can be heard easily.
But the inaudible one can be conceived rhythmically.
The audible music is sweet, but inaudible one is sweeter.
As the former appeals to the ears,
But the latter vibrates the mind with cheers.

If we fail to conceive the inaudible music,
Our life will lose its power of motion.
And will be barren in the true sense of the term.
Just like a River loses its natural flow of water.
When it is shrouded in the Moss.

What is needed to hear the inaudible music?
Is nothing but the rapt attention and the careful mind.
The music of words can be heard with the inner ears-
If we absorbed in ourselves, forgetting near and dear.

Every music has its own rhythmic beauty –
Which may be called its music tune.
Through which we hear the music of words
Which is unique in nature and really a boon.

Music pervaded in the world of cheers.
And gives us pleasure year after year.
It inspires us from our very birth
And soothes our Heart when we depart.

ODE ON THE CREATION OF THE UNIVERSE

The great Creator created this Universe
At His own whims and caprices;
When the desire arose to taste His inner feeling
And to enjoy the beauty being immersed into it.

At first the creator had no companion to play with,
Which vitiates His mind and made Him monotonous.
In order to get rid of the monotony of life
He created the playful unique Universe.
Here lies the birthplace of this great creation
Which is created after His own fashion.

The Almighty loves fun and the Universe is really a funny one.
All of us here are funny in nature like the Father.
And the fun relieves us from the agony of life.
So we feel fresh like that of the engine of a train
That runs mile after mile but knows no rest.
Just like the running horse in the race.

We are here to enjoy the life playfully.
As the Universe in nothing but a playground.
And we are to play here like the players in the game –
Thinking the success and failure of life as the same.

We are here to do our duty entrusted upon us,
Just like the beloved father bestowed on his son.
We are to complete those duties within the framework of life;
Otherwise, it will never be completed
And the Father will rebuke us for our negligence.

ODE ON THE WAYFARER

I am a wayfarer and have no home of my own.
No one asks me from where I come and where to go.
I walk and walk like a vagabond
Descending from the heavenly abode.

I have no lust after name and fame,
As I am a wayfarer by birth.
And travel hither and thither
Preaching His valuable errand.

My life is a running train
And runs as fast as it can.
Just like a galloping horse
Which knows no rest till end.

My duty is to run on the road
Till my legs permit me to go.
And my return journey begins
At the fag-end of my life.

I am free from the bondage of life,
As I am not a family man.
And none shed tears for my death
As I am a bona fide vagabond.

My only aim in life is to reach to the Father
From where I have come to the Earth.
And to remind the people His errand –
"Live and let live in the world with cheers".

ODE ON THE DOOMS DAY

Dooms Day is the day for devastation.
On that day, the people will breathe their last.
And will assemble together before the great Judge
For the final judgment of their virtues and vices on Earth.

On that day, the people will come out of their graves
And awaited eagerly for final judgment.
The criminals will be convicted as per the crimes committed
And will be put into the Hell as per the sections provided.

Those who committed major crime will be sentenced to death
And those committed minor offences
 Will be sentenced to term-imprisonment.
But the pious ones will be acquitted of the charges
And lead a blissful life in the Heaven with Gods and Goddess.

When the conviction is over the prisoners will set free
And will appear before the Almighty Father.
For their future course of actions decided by Him.

He advised them to come down from the Heaven to the Earth
And to lead a harmonious life of eternal bliss,
Where there will be no place of hatred and malice.
The people will think themselves one and the same
And the earth will be transformed into the Heaven.

The new generation will evolve into a Nation
And will work for each other on the basis of selfless interest –
For the benefit of the Humanity as a whole
Where there will be no place for the rich and the poor.
All are equal and aspire after the same goal
In this way, the Earth will be transformed into the Heaven

And none will find any distinction among them.
As all of them belong to the Gods and Goddess –
Rectifying the previous character through punishment.

ODE ON A BIRD OF BEAUTY

I have heard the cuckoo's cooing.
I have heard the bee's humming.
I have heard the wind's blowing.
Which produced the melodious song
And attracts the doleful heart
In such an overwhelming manner
That I remain spellbound to its melodious sound
And cannot utter any word like a hypnotized one.

When I immersed in deep distress,
And cannot find any way to save myself,
The song consoles my mind and gives a new lease of life
To survive in the world for a longer period of time;
Forgetting the sorrows and the sufferings of the past.

But I never heard such a thrilling song
Which replete my heart in such an ecstatic manner
That my mind begins to dance with the sweet music of the song
Forgetting the separate entity between us.

I heard the song of a foreign bird.
As she appeared before my inward eye.
When I lie in my bereaved bed on a solitary night.
She sang a melodious song to soothe my grieved heart
Elevating my mind to a jubilant height.

My doleful heart turns into a joyful one.
When I heard her melodious song,
And begins to dance with joy and harmony
Forgetting the separate entity.

But when I go to catch the bird with my hand
She fled away leaving me in the dreamland.
Where there is none but I to shed tears
Lamenting over year after year.

She is a bird of beauty and inspires at every walk of life
But cannot be seen or touched by hand.
As she is living in the land of the fairies
Where no man can reach in living.

ODE ON THE WINGED WORLD

The birds fly in the sky with the help of the wings.
The fish swims in the river with the help of the fins.
The wind blows on the earth and water with its motion
The earth moves round the sun at its own rotation.

Everything of this world is as free as the wind.
And can move anywhere according to the free will.
None can check the free movement in any way,
As it is the birth right of everyone so to say.

Word is the most powerful phenomenon of this world,
As we cannot express ourselves without the medium.
If there is no word, the world becomes meaningless.
And it remains stagnant and cannot move apace.

The word can fly over the Earth and the Sky.
Just like that of a bird of wings.
If the word cannot fly to convey the message,
The modern civilization will surely come to an end.

The vast world becomes our nearest neighbor,
As we can contact the world within the shortest time.
And express thoughts and feelings with each other
Just like the members of the same family.

It is only possible due to the winged world
Which can fly anywhere in establishing relation.
If the word fails to establish relation between man and man
The world will cease to exist and cannot flourish with its romance.

ODE ON THE RHYTHMS

The world is full of rhythms,
It presents everywhere in some form or other.
And gives us immense pleasure
In molding our life and character.

It acts as the blood circulation of the body.
As, without blood circulation the body cannot exist.
Similarly the world is out of gear,
If the rhythms disappear.
Rhythm is the very basis on which the world is moving.
And gives us a new lease of life to survive.

The raindrops pattered on the ground
Producing a melodious sound.
The river moves towards the ocean
With gentle murmuring motion.

The Earth moves round the Sun like a dancer.
The wind blows gently over the earth and water
Refreshing our fatigued mind in the summer.
The boat danced to the rhythm of the waves
Just like the actor and actress.

The birds twitter in a rhythmic manner.
Which refreshes our mind from the agony of life.
And gives us new energy and vigor
To lead the life with new enthusiasm.

The night comes after the day in a rhythmic way.
The season comes one after another in a cyclic order.
The world proceeds towards the infinity

Following the norms of integrity.
God loves fun and the world is funny enough.
It is the source of inspiration through which we work together.
Forgetting disbelief impending over us
From the very birth to the eternal departure.

Without rhythm we cannot imagine anything,
Even we hear it in our heartbeat
If our heartbeat fails we face imminent death.
Similarly, if there is no rhythm in the world,
The world cannot proceed any further;
And appears before us like a useless corpse.

In this way we feel in everything rhythmic beauty
Which inspires us in every walk of life.
And gives us immense pleasure to survive.
From the very beginning it acts as the nucleus.
And gives us a new dimension towards the perfection.

ODE ON THE VIRGIN FLOWER

Pluck no flower, pluck no flower;
As she sleeps with her Mother.
Touch no more, touch no more;
As her chastity may be devoured.

Molest her not, molest her not;
As she is the source of joy to all.
Kiss no more, kiss no more;
As she may not be as fresh as before.

Her smiling face leads us to the path of progress,
Forgetting the path of malice and hatred.
She consoles our bereaved heart,
When we are in deep distress.

She teaches us the values of life,
Which cannot be purchased from the market;
But to be achieved through self-sacrifice,
Forgetting the racial boundaries.

Love and let love should be the motto of life;
As it acts as the wonderful magic-wand,
To wash away the garbage of mind;
And to give it a new inspiration to serve the mankind.

ODE ON THE METEORIC RISE OF A POLITICIAN

He came of a very common family
With no political background so to say
But he rose very high in the twinkle of an eye
As a mighty meteor in the political sky.

He believed in the "Theory of Activity".
And rose to the prominence through it.
His creativity leads him to the path of prosperity
In molding the life with charming beauty.

His life was full of battles
And he came out successful at the end.
He never frightened to fight in the battle of life
Just like an undaunted solider.

Human life is a wonderful blending of will and woe
Someone succumbed to woes without struggling hard.
And cannot proceed any further;-
Where lies the tragedy of life.

He is a dreadful warrior with a smiling face,
And accepts the life as a challenge of 'No Defeat';-
In the midst of sorrows and sufferings.
He knows well how to overcome the obstacles of life
And hoisted the flag of victory like a gallant soldier
With indomitable courage and valor.

He drinks the life to the lees,
Just like the gallant Ulysses.
And gave it a charming shape-
Through continued stresses and strains.
But all his hopes are nipped in the bud,
When the betrayal bullets of the brother pierced his heart

Which reminds us the famous remark of Julius Caesar;-
"Et-tu, Brute", - my dear

ODE ON A SOBBING DEER

I came across a sobbing deer,
Sobbing to herself, shedding tear after tear.
As she lost her dearest fawn.
In the forest where they lived long.

She tried her best to find out the dearest,
But all her attempts were in vain.
And she remains speechless all the while,
Just like a statue without life.

Tears streamed down her cheeks,
Just like a hilly stream.
Which knows no bounds to flow down,
From the mountain above the ground.

Her tears ran a race with the stream water,
An unequal competition, whatsoever.
I observed the race motionless,
As my grieved heart finds to harbor to rest.
The race came to an end,
When she found her beloved;-
Who kissed her again and again,
With profound love of oneness.

Her grieved Heart melted down,
With the sweetest touch of the beloved.
And she spoke out with a melodious sound-
Sweet, "My beloved", we are to walk many a mile ahead.

ODE ON THE INGREDIENTS OF LIFE

My life is an endless struggle,
And I am to struggle tooth and nail;
To win over the battle of life
And to enjoy the same with valorous strife.

I have no weapon to fight with,
My conscious is my only weapon;
Through which I fight with the enemies,
Just like the mighty Bulldozer.

When fatigue grasped my energy,
And I cannot fight anymore.
My doleful Heart appeared
And showed me the proper road.

Fighting can never be the path of life,
And it can never give us pleasure.
It may be called the Royal Road to Brutality
Where men and women are slaughtered.

Life is not a bed of roses,
But a strange mixture of weal and woe.
We are to accept the life with all its ingredients,
In order to enjoy the life as a whole.

ODE ON THE UPS AND DOWNS OF LIFE

Ups and downs are the very breath of life,
Without it the life cannot be viable.
As we cannot expect the existence of a River
If it has no tidal movement.

The flow-tide overflowed the River with its banks,
And gives it a new lease of life.
To struggle hard for the future;
With indomitable courage and valour.

But the ebb-tide reveals an opposite picture.
It makes the river thinner to thinner.
Just like a diabetic patient of longer period.
Who has lost his energy and vigor.

Similarly, during the rising period of life
The life, seems to be a blooming flower.
And attracts the attention of one and all.
With overwhelming beauty and glamour.
But during falling period of life
The life loses it fragrance and beauty.
And seems to be dull and drudgery.
With no hope to regain for the future.

The proverb, "None but the brave deserves the fair",
Is true to the bottom in our practical life.
If we brave enough to face the adversities of life,
The life will regain its lost hope and aspirations.
And allures our heart like the cherry flowers.

ODE ON THE ABANDONED CHILD

My mother left me alone,
After giving me birth.
My father went to the sea
And never returned.

I am living on the sea-shore,
Throughout the day and night
None showed me any sympathy
As I am an abandoned child.

When I fall in deep distress,
 None come for my help.
How can I lead my life,
Without any help and guide?

Can anyone of you imagine,
What a doleful life I lead?
On the desolated sea-shore
Where I have no relatives.

Tears rolled down from my eyes
Like the hilly fountains.
And drenched my Body and Mind.
When I remind my parents.

ODE ON THE BEAUTY OF THE LAKE

The ducks are swimming in the lake,
The breeze is blowing overhead,
The flowers are distributing sweet smell,
Towards the visitors assembled.

The birds are twittering together,
To refresh themselves from the agony of life.
And dancing on the branches of the trees,
With their respective husbands and wives.

The plants are standing at the gate,
Dressing themselves with colorful dress;
To give a warm reception to those-
Who have come to visit the lake.

What a beautiful scenery the lake presents
Before the lovers of the lake!
Which give them immense pleasure
When they are enjoying the bed.

ODE ON THE HAVE-NOTS

The world is divided into two blocks,
One for the Haves and the other for the Have-nots.
The haves are limited in number
But they enjoy the pomp and grandeur.
Leaving aside the have-nots in the dark-chamber.
Where they lead the life of beggars.

They work from the sunrise to the sunset,
And find no time to take rest.
What a miserable life they lead,
No pen has the power to describe.

After death, they face an acute problem.
As there is no graveyard to bury them.
The vultures come forward as social workers,
And preserved the corpse into their artificial graveyard;-
In order to save the world from the hands of pollution.
What a sacrifice they made to the selfish human-race,
None can express it in language.

ODE ON THE POSTHUMOUS CHILD

Hallow, my dear posthumous child;
Why have you come to this world -
Leaving behind the heaven above?
What gospel have you brought?

Your Father has gone to the Heaven
Leaving behind the Earth beneath.
And you have descended from the Heaven to the Earth
What a wonderful mutual transfer!

There is none to look after you in this Earth
As your mother met death after your birth.
Who will nourish and bring you up
In this sordid world so harsh?

You are surrounded with the ferocious enemy
Who might not show you any sympathy.
How would you maintain existence?
It is really a matter of agony and fear.

ODE ON MISS BEAUTY

I am Miss Beauty, as people called me.
So they visit me frequently to enjoy my beauty.
I am so beautiful to them that they encircled me
Like the bee-hive throughout the day and night.

My body is rosy white, and my face is Pearl-like;
So they come to me to be bathed with my beauty.
Someone called me Cleopatra for my majestic power
And someone called me Helen as I am as beautiful as a Flower.

ODE ON THE BODY AND MIND

Body and Mind are correlated with each other.
We can't expect one leaving behind the other
As we can't imagine a child without its parents;-
So we can't expect the Mind without the Body inherent.

A child can't do anything independently,
Without the guidance of its parents.
Similarly, a Body has no power to move freely
If the Mind cannot cooperate.
The Body moves hither and thither
With the permission of the Mind altogether.

The Mind has the visionary power to do or undo anything
But the Body has no power to imagine,
It always depends upon the suggestions of the Mind.
So it is our Mind who guides us on the path of life.
If the mind does not guide us properly;
Our life will not find its coveted goal.
And will appear before us like the boredom.
Which has no practical implication of its own.

ODE ON OLD AGE

Old age is an age of return journey towards the Heaven –
From where we have come down to this earth
And live a certain period of time
With our feigning Father and Mother.

When we come down to this Earth,
We have come with certain summons to be served;
Within the period of time allotted to us.
Or the Father will be furious enough
And sentenced us to the Hell for disobedience;
Where we have to undergo to the rigorous punishment.
And none will advocate for our bail.
As God is the sole Authority of the Heaven.
And he dictates everything at the helm.

Our mind begins to tremble with fear,
When we remember the last days of our voyage.
And no lame excuse will be granted by God
Because he oversees our activities of the Earth.

ODE ON THE BIRTHDAY CELEBRATION

Birthday should be celebrated year after year,-
With due importance by "Three Cheers".
As it unfolds before us the true picture of life
From the very birth to the present time.

Our life is measured by the Magic-wand of time,-
With all its activities performed and left behind.
We are to perform the activities entrusted upon us,
Within the Panorama of life in this mortal world.
Otherwise, it will never be materialized during the life time,-
And we will be held responsible for our negligence.
Our life will appear before us drudgery and dull,-
Which in no way be called, the life at all.

Our life is the paradise on the Earth,-
And we are the architects of the same.
So we should build it on the firm foundation of fame –
Which will never come to an end.
Just like the 'Taj Mahal' built by Shahjahan, the Great;-
To commemorate the immortal love of his beloved.

ODE ON WEAL AND WOE

Weal and Woe come to everyone in quick succession,
Just like the ebb-tide and the flow-tide of the ocean.
If Woe comes to anyone, can Weal be far behind?
It will naturally come to everyone in due time.

If we do not accept Weal and Woe,
As the natural ingredients of our life.
The life will remain drudgery and dull,
And will not afford us any pleasure.

Weal and Woe make our life enjoyable to us,
And give us complete satisfaction.
Just like the current of the ocean,
Which overflows its banks at its own motion.

If there is no current in the ocean,
The Ocean is presumed to be a dead one.
And cannot be enjoyable to us.
Similarly, a life devoid of pain and pleasure;
Is no longer a life in the true sense of the term.

ODE ON HUMBLE PRAYER TO GOD

God, save us from the danger ahead,
And give us moral courage;
To cope with the struggle of life
Which beset us like a crocodile.

You are our Almighty Father,
And we are your sons and daughters.
So, you are to guide us towards the goal of life,
Defeating the obstacles as the threat to us.
In accomplishing the noble ambition.

We are in the dark of our future,
And do not know what way to follow;-
For the culmination of our life's perfection
Which is our ultimate goal.

You are to guide us as our benevolent Father,
In order to reach at the goal of our life.
Otherwise, all our activities will be nipped in the bud,
And we are to cry in the wilderness at last.

Oh God! Please give us the light of life,
Through which we can see the world around us;
And serve the oppressed humanity at large-
Who are our fellow brothers and sisters.

ODE ON TRUTH AND BEAUTY

Beauty is Truth, Truth Beauty;
There goes the mighty proverb –
Which signifies – truth and Beauty
Are one and the same thing.
Just like the two sides of a coin.

What is beautiful to our eyes,
Will remain visible in our mind;
And leaves a lasting impression of its own
Throughout the whole course of life.

Our inward eyes are the mighty microscope of our life,
Through which we see the invisible into a visible one.
And distinguish between the beauty and the ugliness
Of an object around us.

The beauty of a thing never fades away,
And it remains ever fresh in the casket of our memory till death.
Just like the sweet dreams remains sweet forever
Without any change in character.

ODE ON THE JUDGMENT OF THE PEACOCK THE GREAT

Once I happened to see under the greenwood tree,
A flock of birds assembled together for judgment;
In the criminal court of Mr. Peacock the great –
Who is famous for his unique judgment.

The accused Mr. Crow, allegedly murdered a sparrow;
For which he was brought before the court under arrest-
And stood by the criminal bench during the judgment.

The first witness, Mr. Dove revealed the truth before the judge
And the second witness, Mr. Heron told the same thing as that of the Dove.
So the judge being confirmed sentenced the accused to death;
By pelting stones on him as long as he survived.

ODE ON THE MERRIMENT

Laugh and merriment should be the motto of life,
Without merriment, the life becomes useless,
And cannot proceed ahead;
Due to shortage of fuel.
Just like a river without current-
Cannot proceed towards the sea
As it has no natural flow of water.

Merriment makes our life enjoyable to us
As it has a soothing power of its own –
Without which the life becomes drudgery and dull
And cannot afford us any pleasure.

A life without pleasure is like a plant without flower.
A flowerless plant cannot draw our attention
As it has no charming power,-
And remains neglected in the bower.

ODE ON FREEDOM OF INDIA

Freedom is our birth-right ,-
And no one can deny it.
As it is the spontaneous flow of mind
Originated from the core of the heart.

It gives us a new impetus towards the goal of life,
Just like the birds fly in the sky;
And the rivers flow towards the sea-
Within the natural surroundings of their own.

The British robbed us the right of self-determinations,
And we were under them like the caged-birds;
Without any amenities of life to be flourished ourselves.
What a sacrifice we led during those days!
No one can express it in any language.

At last on the 15th August, 1947; we liberated ourselves,
And came out victorious from the British-bondage;
Forming a sovereign state of our own India by name.
With the power and privilege to govern ourselves
Under our own constitution headed by the president.

ODE ON AN ACT OF KINDNESS

One afternoon, I was wandering in vacant mood;
As I have no work at my disposal.
So, I worked hither and thither
Just like an aimless vessel.

Suddenly, a boy came before me for help.
His mind was overflowing with grief.
As he could not procure his exam-fees –
Due to his extreme poverty.

I looked at the boy with motionless eyes
And found out the agony of his life.
So I helped him with what I had,-
To redress the grief of his mind.

He left the place with a smiling face
Thanking me again and again.
As my help will give him a new lease of life
And he will be able to go in for the examination to be held.

Tears rolled down from my eyes,
Like the summer tempest.
And drenched my body and mind,
Like the water of the holy Ganges.

ODE ON 'FOOD'

Food is essential for the development of body and mind.
Without proper food the body cannot move anywhere;-
As it is the source of energy and moving power;-
Which helps us to reach at the goal of life.

If we do not take food regularly,
Our body becomes weak and feeble.
And we cannot move anywhere.
Just like the engine of a train without fuel.

Food is the source of all sorts of energy.
Without proper food no animal can exist.
Even the trees take food from their Mother Earth
With the help of the roots for their existence.

Now we are to decide what type of food to be taken,-
And what should not be taken at all.
Our conscious says to take the balanced diet;
For balancing the body and mind together.
In order to reach at the goal of life
With tremendous unification of body and mind.

ODE ON THE VILLAGE AND TOWN

God made the village,
And men made the town.
What is the difference between them
Can anyone find it out?

The village appears before us-
With all its original forms and features
And gives us immense pleasure-
Which are the gifts of Almighty Father.

When we enjoy the natural scenery of the village,
Our Mind begins to dance with joy.
As we are breathing the fresh air,
Which is hard to find anywhere.

The villagers are innocent in character,
And lead a very simple life of their own.
They like to entertain the guests as Gods and Goddess.
Which is unbelievable of the people of the Town.

The people of the town present a different picture of their own,
They are self-interested and always think for themselves;
Ignoring the interest of the fellow brethren –
Who are very near and dear to them.

They pose themselves to be the only gentlemen,
And none is allowed to compare with them.
As they are descended from the Heaven,-
With their separate entity and embellishment.

What a sharp contrast we find,-
Between the two sections of people!

One is centered round for their own interest
But the other is devoted to serve the fellow brethren.

ODE ON A PEN

I am a little fountain Pen,
As people called me by this name.
But I have the magnetic power of my own,
Through which I can conquer the heart of the people
And win the battle of life defeating the brute force.

War is not at all a peaceful solution of a problem,
As it welcomes another war to take revenge of the same.
So the Second World War is the outcome of the first one
Which is more devastating in nature than that of the former.

Peaceful negotiation is the only path to solve the problem
Which is only possible through the brainwork of the mighty Pen.
So, there goes the proverb, 'Pen is mightier than the Sword',
As it has a wonderful soothing power of its own.

ODE ON THE HERMITAGE

Hermitage is the abode of the Hermits-
Where the monks or the retired persons assembled together,
In order to avoid the din and bustle of the family life-
For which they dedicated themselves for its improvement,
But all their efforts are gone in vain.

Accordingly to the Hindu Mythology, this life is called
'Vanaprastha'.
The third stage of life, where the people come after the
'Brahmacharya' and 'Grihastha'.
The Grihastha is the most crucial life of the human beings,
Where they live with their near and dear ones,-
And left no stone unturned for its entire development,
But alas! They find no credit for the same.

So they prefer Vanaprastha as their ultimate goal,
Where they devote themselves whole-heartedly to the prayer
of the Almighty;
Who is the sole solace after the retirement.
As they have been deprived off all amenities of life.

ODE ON THE VIRGIN FLOWER

One day when I was walking along the road side,
Suddenly I came across a rose garden-
Where various types of roses bloomed
With their various colors in the noon.

They were singing and dancing together,
With their mirthful enjoyment of the youth.
Which enchanted my eyes in such a manner-
That I remained spellbound and could not produce any sound.
Just like a hypnotized one, who has no sense at all.

I forgot my entity and began to dance with them
As they are my bosom friends.
But when I ran to touch them, they became an emblem
And dictated me not to touch them.
As beauty is to see not to touch.
If you touch the Beauty, the Beauty loses its purity
And turns into a common commodity of no importance.

ODE ON THE FLOOD

People called me flood – as I flooded the earth with water;-
Making the same unfit for human habitation.
I come to the Earth from the Heaven above
To punish the people for their committed crimes
As they are disobedient to the Heavenly Father
Who fosters them with all sorts of amusement.
For the all-round development of the life.

The world is the 'paradise of peace'-
Where people should live peacefully
And try to make the world into the Heaven above;
With their peaceful co-existence and self-sacrifice.

But what we see in practice?-
The world is beset with ferocious beasts,-
And always fighting with each other
To fulfill their personal greed.

When they fail to fulfill their greed
They behave like the ferocious beasts.
And began to fight with each other-
Turning the human habitation into the den of the beasts.
Where there is no love and peace
But full of animosity and greed.

The Heavenly Father tried his best
To rectify the Human race.
But all His attempts are gone in vain.
As they are totally disobedient.

So He becomes very angry with the people of the world
And sends me on the Earth to teach them a good lesson.

I flooded them with all their belongings into the water
As soon as they satisfy the Heavenly Father-
With deep love and humble submission.

ODE ON THE BEAUTY OF DARKNESS

Have you witnessed the beauty of darkness-
Which generally seen at the dead of night?
When people are in sound sleep
And the nature is calm and quiet.

It appears before us as the Goddess of Night
Absorbed in deep meditation.
In order to bring back the Sunny days on the Earth
For the benefit of the humanity at large.

At dead of night, when the nature is calm and quiet
The darkness of Night appears before us as the night of romance
Which leads us towards the goal of life with its various taste and colors.
Depending on the wings of romantic imagination.

If there is no romance in our life,
The life appears before us drudgery and dull;
And cannot proceed any further for its unification
Which is the ultimate goal of our life.

ODE ON THE MONKEY MIND

Our life is the 'Battle-Field' of continuous Fighting;-
So we are to fight throughout the life for our existence.
If we fail to win over the 'battle of life' –
Our life will be doomed and never be bloomed.

Our mind is the commander-in-chief in the 'battle of life'
And guides us towards the fulfillment of our hopes and aspirations;-
Defeating the obstacles which prevent our advancement towards the goal.
So, we are to give 'free-hand' to the mind for winning the 'battle of life'.
Otherwise, all of our hopes and aspirations will be nipped in the bud-
Due to non-cooperation of the five generals entrusted upon.
Who may even revolt against the mind for neglecting them in the battle;
And threatened the same for bare consequence.

The mind is also guided by three generals of opposite characters,-
They are 'SATTVA, RAJAS and TAMAS' by name and fame.
The 'SATTVA' guides the Mind towards the purity and light.
The 'RAJAS' guides the Mind towards the pomp and power.
But the 'TAMAS' guides the Mind towards inertia and despair.
All of them put pressure on the Mind to fulfill their demands at the same time.
How the mind will reconcile them and come out victorious in the battle?
Being nervous, the Mind begins to swing from one to another-
Just like the confused Monkey from one branch of the tree to the other.

ODE ON CO-OPERATION

Co-operation leads us towards the creation;
Creation leads us towards the perfection.
Without perfection the life has no charm of its own,
And cannot proceed towards the goal;-
Which in no way be called, the life at all.
As it has lost the power of creativity,
Which makes the life enliven to us.
For its active participation in the field of creation.

Without creative activities, the life appears before us;
Like a current less river without any motion;-
Which cannot follow towards the ocean
Though it has plenty of water.

If there is no cooperation, there is no creation;
And both of them are so correlated with each other-
That we cannot expect their separate existence
Just like the twins of their same mother.
Who are exactly resembled with each other-
In their original forms and features.
So it may rightly be called "The Golden Key",
To open the door of the creativity.

If we look at the beautiful Nature around us,
We are surprised to see its unique beauty;-
Which enchanted our mind in such an ecstatic way
That we cannot express it in any language;-
Which is also the gift of Nature bestowed upon us
Through the co-operation of our sensual organs.

THE EPILOGUE

In the epilogue, I would like to mention that I have composed the odes on various topics of our social and cultural life with varied tastes and flavors, which come upon my mind during the leisure hours of my life. I have given them thorough expression with lucid and vivid manner to the best of my ability. I feel intense delighted if my earnest labor in the composing of odes be crowned with success in the wining of hearts of the readers in general for whom the odes are composed of.

www.ingramcontent.com/pod-product-compliance
Lightning Source LLC
Chambersburg PA
CBHW022114040426
42450CB00006B/692